Bridges of Venice

Walking Tours

Every effort has been made to ensure the accuracy of the information included in this book. Renovation, maintenance, and other changes frequently happen in the world of travel. As a result, the author cannot accept responsibility for inaccurate information or for inadvertent errors or omissions. The author cannot accept responsibility for any consequences arising from the use of this book.

ISBN 978-0-6152-1958-5

First Edition

This book is dedicated to my two sons, Brian and Brad. They, being parents themselves, know the bond between father and child.

Also available by James Broos

Venice Bridges
A Pictorial Collection

400 Full Color Photographs

Visit www.jamesbroos.com for the
latest information about current and
future books authored by James Broos.

Yea the lines hast thou laid unto me
in pleasant places,
And the beauty of this thy Venice
has thou shown unto me
Until is its loveliness become unto me
a thing of tears.

O God, what great kindness
have we done in times past
and forgotten it,
That thou givest this wonder unto us,
O God of waters? ...

Yea, the glory of the shadow
of thy Beauty hath walked
Upon the shadow of the waters
In this thy Venice. ...

O God of waters,
make clean our hearts within us
And our lips to show forth thy praise.
For I have seen the
Shadow of this thy Venice
Floating upon the waters,

And thy stars
Have seen this thing out of their far-courses
Have they seen this thing,
O God of waters.

Even as are thy stars
Silent unto us in their far-coursing,
Even so is mine heart
become silent within me.

Ezra Pound
Night Litany, *1908*

5

Contents

Introduction
    History   9
    General   12

Why Tour the Bridges   13

Bridge Numbers and Names   15

Special Bridges   19

Bridge Tours   31

Photographs of the Bridges   89

Some Interesting Bridge Facts   140

Travel Information and Tips   141

Acknowledgments   145

Index   146

INTRODUCTION

History

Complete books have been written about the history of Venice. This section introduces only a few of the highlights of Venice's past.

Sixteen centuries ago the beginnings of Venice emerged out of mud flats in a shallow lagoon. Many historians believe the official beginning of Venice was in the year 421. Around the year 452 Attila the Hun was ravaging many sections of Italy. This event caused a major exodus to the various islands of what was to become Venice.

From almost the very beginning Venetians felt the need to have a saint to protect them and guide their lives. Their first patron saint was St. Theodore. In 828 St. Mark became their lasting patron saint. His mummified body was stolen from Alexandria and smuggled into Venice. It is said his body is buried in St. Mark's Basilica.

Most Venetian historians agree the current church is the third St. Mark's Basilica to be constructed on the site. The first St. Mark's Basilica was consecrated in 832. This church was heavily damaged by fire in the late 900's and a second structure was built. Then in 1063 construction began on the current basilica.

Entrance to St. Mark's is free, however small fees are charged to visit several important areas within the church. One such area not to be missed is where the Pala d'Oro (Gold Altarpiece) resides. It was created in the tenth century and contains hundreds of jewels.

The growing Venetian empire possessed a strong military force and developed excellent battle tactics, both on sea and on land. During the eighth century, Venice found itself in a dangerous situation. The Franks, led by the son of Charlemagne, invaded the Venetian lagoon. They advanced to the capital of Venice and laid siege to it. The Venetians moved their capital to Rivo Alto (present-day Rialto area). The battle that followed demonstrated the cunning of the Venetian military leaders.

Venice's naval forces led the Franks into a narrow channel. Then the Venetians lured the Franks away from their ships and onto a low island composed mostly of sand. The two military forces engaged in a battle on the island until the tide was well on its way out.

Soon low tide had closed the entrance to the channel and the ships of the Franks were stranded. At this stage of the battle more Venetians arrived, this time in flat bottom boats. They rescued their fellow citizens from the island and destroyed the Franks' ships. With no means of escape, the Franks' fighting force remaining on the island drowned as high tide covered their battleground with water!

Venice is well known for romance and intrigue. In the year 944 twelve brides were having a combined wedding when pirates from Trieste forced their way into the church. The brides (along with their dowries) were kidnapped. The Venetian grooms and guests at the wedding soon pursued the kidnappers, killing them and returning the brides and their dowries to Venice.

By the year 1200 Venice had established itself as a world power in trading. Born in Venice, Marco Polo set out on his epic journey to China in 1271. There he became good friends with Kublai Khan and served the great leader in numerous capacities. Marco left China in 1292. Bridge Tour 5 of this book takes you to the neighborhood where Marco Polo grew up.

The year 1576 saw Venice engulfed by the Bubonic plague. Estimates range from 40,000 to 70,000 Venetians who were killed by this disease. The Redentore Basilica was built on the island of Giudecca to give thanks for the ending of the plague. Then in 1630 the plague struck again, killing about 45,000 Venetians. To commemorate the end of this plague, the church Santa Maria della Salute was constructed. This massive basilica stands as one of the prime examples of Venetian ingenuity. The construction of this church required 1,156,627 wooden piles to be driven into the mud for the foundation.

One of the oldest surviving cafés in Italy, Café Florian, was opened in Venice in 1720 and is located in St. Mark's Square. The food and drink are moderately expensive, but a person should not miss the opportunity to sip a cup of coffee in the old-world charm of this café. Café Florian is the oldest café in Venice.

The year 1797 is generally held to mark the fall of the Venetian Empire. Napoleon gained control of Venice but soon ceded the city to the Austrian Empire. In 1866 Venice gained its independence from Austrian rule and became part of a unified Italy. Venice was spared any bomb damage from the two world wars. This fact makes Venice somewhat unique considering the large number of important cities in Europe that were heavily damaged by bombing attacks.

Tourism is by far the largest industry in Venice today. Visit this city during the summer months or during Carnevale in February and it seems to literally overflow with people.

The streets of Venice do sometimes flood, rarely however does the water rise to the level it did in 1966. The severity of that flood prompted numerous control measures and studies to determine the most feasible ways to prevent a future major flood. You should not let the threat of a flood prevent you from visiting Venice. I have visited Venice many times and have encountered high water on only one occasion.

Prior to my first visit to Venice, I had only a small interest in classical music. In late September of 1983 I sat alone at a café table in St. Mark's Square. My wife and two young sons were indeed far away in North Carolina. As I wished to be near them, a sidewalk orchestra was performing a classical composition I later discovered was Vivaldi's Four Seasons. Somehow Vivaldi knew, 300 years earlier, how to compose a concerto to ease my pain of loneliness!

Antionio Vivaldi (1678 – 1741) composed over 600 concertos. His most famous work is indeed the "Four Seasons". He was made musical director of the La Pietà church in 1703. The church was an orphanage for girls and they performed in his orchestra and choir. La Pietà church is included in Bridge Tour 6.

General

Venice is a city like no other. There seems to be an endless number of streets, however no motorized vehicles or bicycles are allowed on them. The common modes of transportation are boats and walking. Certainly the best way to see Venice for the first time is by water craft from the train station or vehicle parking area down the Grand Canal to St. Mark's Square.

Venice has approximately 410 bridges. This number changes from time to time for various reasons. Canals (or portions of canals) are sometimes filled in to create additional space for walking or buildings. New (occasionally private) bridges are built in the city. Certain bridges may be under renovation and therefore unavailable for public use (or view). For these reasons as you engage in the bridge tours of this book, you may discover bridges not included here or come upon bridges that you are unable to see or cross. This situation may require you to alter the directions listed in a bridge tour. Be flexible!

A new bridge has been constructed across the Grand Canal near Piazzale Roma and the train station. It is constructed primarily of steel. The bridge is named Ponte di Calatrava after its Spanish designer. This is the fourth bridge to span the Grand Canal.

This city is composed of over one hundred islands and one hundred and seventy canals. Approximately three thousand streets and alleys are located in Venice. It is easy to get lost in this city, but you should not let this frighten you. Remember that you are on an island. If you lose your way, a walk of only a few minutes will usually place you at a sign pointing in the direction of one of the major gathering areas of the city (i.e. San Marco, Rialto, Ferrovia [train station], Piazzale Roma [vehicle parking]). More detailed information is included in the section titled "Travel Information and Tips".

Why Tour the Bridges

The city of Venice is filled with priceless paintings, amazing architecture, numerous awe-inspiring sights, and seemingly more than our senses can absorb. So why should a person spend time going from bridge to bridge using a guide book and following pre-determined directions? A bridge is just a bridge, right? Wrong! The bridges have an allure all their own.

As you visit these bridges it is easy to place yourself back in time to the glory, romance, and intrigue that was old Venice! Marco Polo's home was located near the square around San Giovanni Crisostomo church. Bridge Tour 5 gives you detailed information about where Marco Polo lived.

Tour 26 is based on the island of Murano. The bridges are somewhat common, however as you visit these bridges you will pass numerous exquisite glass shops. Murano glass is world famous for its beauty and craftsmanship. If you have the time, be sure to visit at least one of the glass blowing areas.

The island of Burano is famous for handmade lace. The lace is indeed beautiful but the island has much more to offer. The houses are the most colorful in all of Venice. Legend has it that the houses were painted such bright and different colors so the fishermen could identify their homes while at sea.

This island has one main commercial area. Located here are numerous shops and several restaurants. Be aware of one important fact; the restaurants often close early compared to other European and American establishments. Notice the leaning tower at one end of the market area.

The island of Torcello does have one very interesting bridge. It is nicknamed the "devil's bridge". To get to this island by using the vaporetto, you must first travel to Burano, then take another vaporetto to Torcello. The first settlement of Venice was actually on this remote island.

Being familiar with certain terms will prove helpful as you follow the directions found in the bridge tours. A Calle is a street. A Campo is a square. The prefix of Ruga means a large street with stores. Sottoportego denotes an arched walkway under a building. Rio terrà defines a canal that has been filled in. Fondamenta signifies a wide street beside a canal. And of course Ponte indicates a bridge. Some Italian words in this book appear to be in the wrong case, especially in bridge names. Examples of this situation are the words dei, di, del, and degli. They are correctly presented as lower case.

As you encounter each bridge, give your senses a workout. There's more to Venice than simply pleasing the eye. Feel the cool, gentle breeze inside a dark portico. Savor the exquisite smell of freshly baked Italian bread and home-made perfumed soap! Give a quick, shy glance at the newly hung laundry flirting with the breeze blowing through the alley.

Hear the sound of operatic voices or Vivaldi's "Four Seasons" as you stand on a little, obscure bridge far off the beaten path of tourists. Listen to the small, unceasing waves as they gently strike the foundations of buildings, having done so for century upon century. Stand by a very old yet beautiful bridge in a seemingly isolated area of the city and soak up the only sound you can hear, that being the church bells ringing over the whole city of Venice! Once the bells cease, the only sound you hear is water. No people, cars, etc. Just this spot as it was 1,000 years ago.

Allow your taste buds to discover the hidden flavors found in Gelato. Feel the exquisite hand-made lace found on the tiny island of Burano. Take the 5 minute vaporetto ride from Burano to the isolated island of Torcello, the origin of Venice.

The numbers assigned to each bridge are my own creation. They are used solely to help identify each bridge. The bridge tours in this book will provide you with an avenue to discover numerous aspects of Venice that few tourists will ever experience. Set yourself apart from the hordes of visitors that see only a tiny fraction of the true majesty of this city!

Bridge Numbers with Names That Are Visible

1 Ponte Della Paglia	
2 Ponte dei Sospiri	14 Ponte S. Maurizio
15 Ponte Vitturi	18 Ponte Giustinian
20 Ponte dell' Accademia	24 Ponte De L'Albero
25 Ponte Michiel	31 Ponte De La Cortesia
34 Ponte Dei Fuseri	36 Ponte De Piscina
37 Ponte De Le Colonne	40 Ponte Dei Dai
43 Ponte De Le Balote	44 Ponte De Le Pignate
45 Ponte Del Lovo	50 Ponte De La Malvasia
52 Ponte De La Guerra	59 Ponte Dei Carmini
60 Ponte De La Corona	61 Ponte Storto
64 Ponte Pasqualigo E Avogadro	70 Ponte De Rugagiuffa
71 Ponte De Le Bande	72 Ponte Del Mondo Novo
73 Ponte De La Fava	74 Ponte S. Antonio
75 Ponte del Rialto	76 Ponte De L'Olio
77 Ponte Marco Polo	78 Ponte Del Pistor
82 Ponte Del Paradiso	83 Ponte Dei Preti
84 Ponte Marcello O Pindemonte	85 Ponte Borgoloco
86 Ponte Tetta	87 Ponte Cappello
88 Ponte S. Lorenzo	89 Ponte Novo
90 Ponte S. Severo	91 Ponte Lion
92 Ponte Dei Greci	94 Ponte Del Diavolo
95 Ponte De La Pieta'	96 Ponte Del Sepolcro
97 Ponte De La Pieta'	98 Ponte S. Antonia
99 Ponte De La Comenda	100 Ponte De La Corte Nova
101 Ponte Del Fontego	102 Ponte De S. Francesco O Del Nuncio
103 Ponte De S. Francesco O Del Nescio	104 Ponte Del Suffragio O Del Cristo
105 Ponte De La Scoazzera	106 Ponte Dei Scudi
107 Ponte De L'Arco	108 Ponte De La Grana
109 Ponte Storto	110 Ponte Dei Penini

111 Ponte De L' Inferno	112 Ponte Del Purgatorio
113 Ponte Erizzo	114 Ponte Ca Di Dio
117 Ponte De L'Arsenal O Del Paradiso	119 Ponte De La Tana
120 Ponte Nuovo	121 Ponte S. Gioachin
122 Ponte Rielo	124 Ponte S. Ana
128 Ponte S. I Sepo	135 Ponte Novo S. Felice
136 Ponte Ubaldo Belli	137 Ponte Privli
140 Ponte S. Caterina	141 Ponte Molin De La Racheta
142 Ponte S. Andrea	143 Ponte Corrente
144 Ponte De Le Vele	145 Ponte Priuli
147 Ponte S. Giovanni Grisostomo	149 Ponte Giustinian
150 Ponte Dei Sartori	151 Ponte De L' Acquavita
152 Ponte Dei Gesuiti	153 Ponte Dona'
154 Ponte Panada	155 Ponte Mendicanti
156 Ponte Cavallo	157 Ponte De La Panada
158 Ponte Del Piovan O Del Volto	159 Ponte S. Maria Novo
160 Ponte Widmann	161 Ponte Pasqualigo
162 Ponte Dei Miracoli	164 Ponte E Calle De Le Erbe
165 Ponte Del Cristo	167 Ponte Dei Conzafelzi
168 Ponte De L' Ospealeto	171 Ponte Fondamenta Di S. Giustina
173 Ponte dei Tre Archi	174 Ponte del Batelo
176 Ponte De Canaregio	177 Ponte De Gheto Vechio
178 Ponte De Gheto Novo	179 Ponte De Gheto Novo
180 Ponte De Le Torete	181 Ponte S. Girolamo
182 Ponte De Le Capuzzine	183 Ponte Moro
185 Ponte Contarini	186 Ponte Turlona
187 Ponte Bonaventura	188 Ponte S. Alvise
189 Ponte De La Malvasia	190 Ponte Dei Ormesini
191 Ponte Loredan	192 Ponte De L' Aseo
193 Ponte Dei Lustraferi	195 Ponte Del Forno
196 Ponte Rosso O Dei Trasti	197 Ponte Brazzo

198 Ponte Dei Mori	199 Ponte Dei Muti
200 Ponte De La Saca	201 Ponte De La Madona De L'Orto
202 Ponte Storto	203 Ponte De L' Anconeta
205 Ponte Correr	206 Ponte De L' Ogio
207 Ponte Nicolo Pasovaligo	208 Ponte Vendramin
209 Ponte S. Fosca	210 Ponte S. Antonio
211 Ponte Diedo	212 Ponte Moro
213 Ponte Zancani	215 Ponte Corte Vechia
217 Ponte De La Misericordia	220 Ponte De La Crea
224 Ponte degli Scalzi	227 Ponte De S. Maria Maggior
229 Ponte De Ca' Rizzi	232 Ponte Del Pagan
234 Ponte De La Cereria	235 Ponte De La Sbiaca
239 Ponte Dei Guardiani	241 Ponte Storto
242 Ponte De La Madona	244 Ponte De Le Terese
245 Ponte De S. Nicolo'	249 Ponte De La Madalena
250 Ponte De S. Sebastian	251 Ponte De S. Basegio
252 Ponte Mounn	253 Ponte Dell' Abazia
256 Ponte Del Umilta'	260 Ponte S. Cristoforo
261 Ponte Del Formager	265 Ponte Deilina Calcina
267 Ponte Longo	268 Ponte De La Scoasera
269 Ponte Trevisan	270 Ponte S. Trovaso
271 Ponte Delle Maravegie	272 Ponte Del Squero
273 Ponte Lombardo	274 Ponte Delle Turchette
279 Ponte Sartorio	281 Ponte Ognisanti
282 Ponte S. Barnaba	283 Ponte Dei Pugni
285 Ponte Foscarini	286 Ponte Del Socorso
287 Ponte Briati	289 Ponte Del Forno
292 Ponte S. Pantalon	293 Ponte Vinanti
294 Ponte Marcello	295 Ponte Del Gafaro
296 Ponte Dei Squartai	299 Ponte Dei Tolentini
302 Ponte De La Berg	303 Ponte Cappello O Dei Garzoti
304 Ponte Canal	306 Ponte De Le Sechere
307 Ponte Del Cristo	308 Ponte De Le Oche

309 Ponte De L' Anatomia	310 Ponte Ruga Bella O Del Forner
311 Ponte Del Savio	312 Ponte Del Megio
313 Ponte Del Tentor	314 Ponte Giovanelli
317 Ponte De La Rioda	318 Ponte Del Cristo O Del Tentor
320 Ponte Colombo	321 Ponte Storto
322 Ponte Del Modena	323 Ponte S. Boldo
324 Ponte Del Parucheta	325 Ponte Bernardo
326 Ponte Del Forner	327 Ponte De L' Agnella
328 Ponte De Le Tette	329 Ponte S. Maria Mater Domini
330 Ponte Giovanni Andrea De La Croce O De La Malvasia	332 Ponte De La Chiesa
333 Ponte Del Ravano	334 Ponte Del Forner
335 Ponte Pesaro	337 Ponte De Le Becarie
338 Ponte De Le Do Spade	339 Ponte Raspi O Sansoni
340 Ponte Storto	341 Ponte De La Furatola
342 Ponte Cavalli	343 Ponte S. Polo
344 Ponte Dei Meloni	345 Ponte De La Madoneta
346 Ponte De La Frescada	348 Ponte Foscari
349 Ponte S. Rocco	350 Ponte Della Scuola
351 Ponte Dei Frari	353 Ponte S. Stin
354 Ponte De Ca' Dona'	355 Ponte S. Agostin
356 Ponte Del Traghetto	357 Ponte De La Croce
359 Ponte Longo	360 Ponte S. Angelo
361 Ponte De Le Scuole	362 Ponte De La Palada
363 Ponte Picolo	364 Ponte S. Eufemia
367 Ponte Lagoscuro	370 Ponte Dei Lavraneri
372 Ponte Angelo Zaniol	373 Ponte De Le Terese
374 Ponte S. Martin	375 Ponte S. Donato
376 Ponte Longo	377 Ponte S. Pietro Martire
378 Ponte De Mezo	379 Ponte S. Chiara
390 Ponte del Diavolo	392 Ponte di Calatrava

Special Bridges

Bridge 2, Ponte dei Sospiri (Bridge of Sighs)

Ponte dei Sospiri was built between 1595 and 1600. This bridge connects the Doge's Palace with the new prisons. The old prisons were located in the Doge's Palace. The bridge's name stems from the fact that prisoners would "sigh" as they crossed it, knowing they were either going to prison or to the courts that would likely place them there.

Bridge 20, Ponte dell' Accademia

The first Accademia Bridge was built in 1854 by the Austrians. It was made of iron. The current wooden bridge was built in 1932.

Bridge 75, Ponte del Rialto

Ponte del Rialto is photographed more than any other bridge in Venice. The Bridge of Sighs (# 2) is a close second in terms of popularity. These two bridges were designed by the same man, Antonio da Ponte.

The original wooden Rialto Bridge was the first structure to span the Grand Canal. It was built in 1264. Like the current bridge, but on a much smaller scale, retail shops were allowed to operate on its length. These shops were closed in approximately 1290. Human traffic and the effects of nature took their toll on the bridge.

The second Rialto Bridge was constructed in 1432. Interestingly enough, the bridge was dismantled and put back together in 1458. Integral to this bridge were the rows of shops found on each side. Several renovations were completed on the structure over a period of 60+ years.

In 1524 a section of the Rialto Bridge fell into the Grand Canal. The bridge was patched and continued in use while the Venetian government studied the feasibility of constructing a stone bridge to replace it.

Many plans were submitted for the new stone bridge. The new structure was required to be in harmony with the surrounding architecture, to be highly functional, and to demonstrate to the world Venice's wealth and creativity. Most drawings included multiple arches for the bridge's support system.

Antonio da Ponte's proposal for the Rialto Bridge consisted of only one arch. His design eventually won approval and the current Rialto Bridge was completed in 1591. The foundations required 6,000 piles to be driven into the ground on each side of the Grand Canal. Then timbers were laid on top of the piles to create a platform. Oak, larch, and alder wood were used for the piles and the platform timbers. Stones were then placed as the top layer.

The drawing on the following page depicts how the current Rialto Bridge was constructed. The long pilings nearest the water were driven in the ground first to form a bulkhead and therefore hold back the waters of the Grand Canal so that a dry area was created to lay the platforms and masonry.

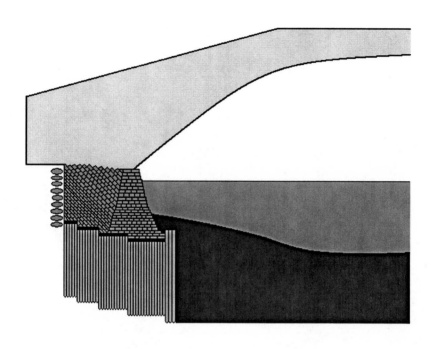

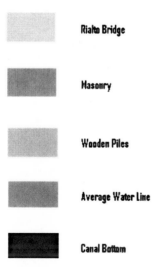

Rialto Bridge

Masonry

Wooden Piles

Average Water Line

Canal Bottom

23

Bridge 82, Ponte Del Paradiso

At one end of the bridge, within the arch above, is a fabulous representation of the Virgin Mary with two small figures by her feet. To each side of the figures are the coats of arms of two prominent Venetian families.

Bridge 107, Ponte De L' Arco

This was the first bridge in Venice to be made of stone and to have an arch.

Bridge 173, Ponte dei Tre Archi

This is the only bridge in Venice with more than one arch.

Bridge 224, Ponte degli Scalzi

In 1860 the Austrians built an iron bridge at this point on the Grand Canal. The current Ponte degli Scalzi was constructed in 1934. This bridge is located beside the train station.

Bridge 283, Ponte Dei Pugni

This bridge is known as the "Bridge of Fists". Ponte Dei Pugni was used by rival clans to stage fist fights during part of the 1600's. Visitors can see the pair of marked footprints where the two fighters stood at the beginning of a contest. Losers of the fights were thrown into the canal. Many people died as a result of the fighting. In 1705 a ban was imposed that stopped the fist fighting. For many years a boat has docked beside the bridge, selling fresh fruit and vegetables.

Bridge 390, Ponte del Diavolo

This bridge is on the Island of Torcello. Centuries ago bridges without railings were common in Venice. Now it is rare to find a Venetian bridge without any railings. Ponte del Diavolo is nicknamed the devil's bridge.

Bridge 392, Ponte di Calatrava

Ponte di Calatrava is the newest bridge across the Grand Canal.
Construction was completed in 2008. Composition of and the need for
this new bridge spanning the "main street" of Venice was debated for
many years. It provides an interesting contrast to the preponderance of
stone and wood bridges.

BRIDGE TOURS

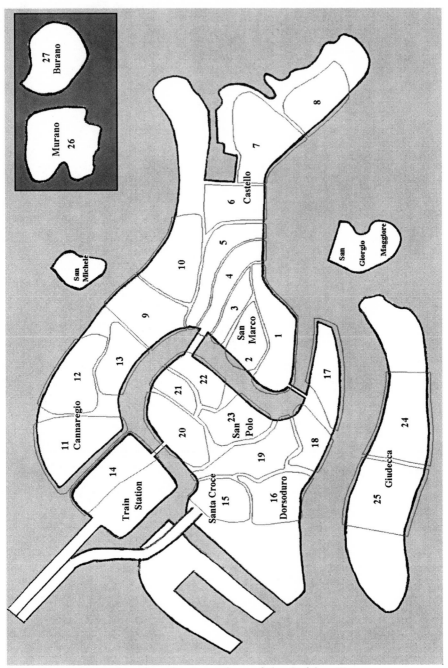

Map Showing the Location of the Bridge Tours

32

Table of Bridge Tours

27 Tours.
Start & End Locations are Vaporetto stops except
St. Mark's Square in Tours 2 & 3 and Rialto Bridge
in Tours 4 & 5.

Tour	Start Location	Start Bridge	End Bridge	End Location	Total Bridges
1	San Zaccaria Paglia	1	23	Sant' Angelo	23
2	Sant' Angelo	24	40	St. Mark's Square	17
3	St. Mark's Square	40	57	St. Mark's Square	18
4	San Zaccaria Danieli	58u	75	Rialto Bridge	19
5	Rialto Bridge	76	95	San Zaccaria Monumento	20
6	San Zaccaria Monumento	96	114	Arsenale	19
7	Arsenale	115	126	Giardini	12
8	Giardini	127	134	Sant' Élena	8
9	Ca' d' Oro	135	153	Fondamenta Nove	19
10	Fondamenta Nove	154	172	Ospedale Civile	19
11	Tre Archi	173	187	Sant' Alvise	15
12	Sant' Alvise	188	201	Madonna dell' Orto	14
13	San Marcuola	202	217	Ca' d' Oro	16
14	Tre Archi	218	224	Ferrovia degli Scalzi	7
15	Piazzale Roma	225	233	Piazzale Roma	9
16	Piazzale Roma	234	252	San Basilio	19
17	Salute	253	267	Záttere Ponte Lungo	15
18	Záttere Ponte Lungo	268	281	Cá Rezzónico	14
19	Cá Rezzónico	282	301	Piazzale Roma	20
20	Ferrovia degli Scalzi	302	313	San Stae	12
21	San Stae	314	335	San Stae	22
22	Rialto	336	345	San Silvestro	10
23	San Tomà	346	356	San Tomà	11
24	Redentore	357	363	Palanca Giudecca	7
25	Palanca Giudecca	364	370	Sacca Fisola	7
26	Venièr	371	379	Colonna	9
27	Burano	380	392	Burano	13

Important Landmarks and the Tours They Are In

Landmark	Tour #
Accademia Galleria	1
Bridge of Sighs	1
Café Florian	3
Campanile	1
Ca' d' Oro	9
Doge's Palace (Palazzo Ducale)	1
Ferrovia (Train Station)	14
Gondola Repair Shop	17
Jewish Ghetto	11
La Fenice Opera House	2
Leaning Towers	2, 27
Madonna dell' Orto Church	12
Marco Polo's Neighborhood	5
Peggy Guggenheim Museum	17
Piazzale Roma	15
Redentore Church	24
Rialto Bridge	4, 22
Rialto Market	22
Santa Maria della Salute Church	17
Santa Maria Formosa Church	4
Santa Maria Gloriosa dei Frari Church	23
Santo Stefano Church	1, 2
St. Mark's Basilica	3
St. Mark's Square	1, 2, 3
Vivaldi's Church	6

This tour contains 23 bridges. It begins at the San Zaccaria Paglia vaporetto stop near St. Mark's Square and ends at the Sant Ángelo vaporetto stop about half way between the Accademia Bridge and the Rialto Bridge.

Start at San Zaccaria Paglia vaporetto stop. There are numerous water bus stops here. Orient yourself so that the statue of the swordsman on a horse is on your right as you stand near the water facing the row of buildings. Turn left and go to the bridge that, once you are on top of it, you will see the Bridge of Sighs visible on your right. You are standing on bridge 1. This bridge is named Ponte de Páglia. The Bridge of Sighs (Ponte dei Sospiri) is bridge 2. It was built between 1595 and 1600.

The Bridge of Sighs connects the Doge's Palace with the new prisons. The old prisons were located in the Doge's Palace. The bridge's name stems from the fact that prisoners would "sigh" as they crossed it, knowing they were either going to prison or to the courts that would likely place them there. Other bridges can also be seen in the distance beyond the Bridge of Sighs.

Cross bridge 1 and walk along the water's edge past St. Mark's Square. Just beyond this famous square you will notice a quiet little park on the right. Continue on and you will be at bridge 3 on the Fondamenta delle Farine. Cross bridge 3 and turn right on Calle Vallaresso. When this street dead ends turn left. Go straight and soon you will cross bridge 4.

Continue on this large street (Calle larga 22 Marzo) to the 2nd street on the right. Turn right on it (Calle del Sartor Da Veste) and go straight to bridge 5.

From bridge 5 backtrack on Calle del Sartor Da Veste to Calle larga 22 Marzo. Upon reaching this wide street, turn right on it and bear to the left and then to the right to bridge 6. On the left is bridge 7, a relatively new bridge. Cross bridge 6 and turn right with the church on your left. Go to the 3rd street on the right (Fondamenta Fenice) along side a canal. Bridge 8 is on your right. On the left you can see bridge 9.

Do not cross bridge 8 or 9. Go back on Calle Del Piovan O Gritti until you arrive at the church. Walk past the Santa Maria Giglio church. Turn right at the corner of this church and you will see bridge 10 on the left and bridge 11 on the right.

Go across bridge 11 and you will see bridge 12 in front of you. Go across bridge 12 and immediately turn right and you will come to bridge 13. Do not cross bridge 13. Turn around and go back toward bridge 12. Take the first right onto Calle Zaguri. Walk straight through Campo S. Maurizio and onto Calle delle Spezièr in the far right corner.

Now you will see bridge 14. Cross it and keep straight. You will get to a large open area (Campo Francesco Morosini). Walk to the far left side and you will see bridge 15, Ponte Vitturi, on your right. Don't cross it, go back to the Campo and turn right, walking around the church. You will make a right turn and see bridges 16, 17, 18 and 19. Do not cross them, but look left and you will see the large Accademia Bridge (bridge 20). This bridge is one of only four bridges that cross the Grand Canal. The Accademia Galleria is on the other side of this bridge.

Walk to the middle of the Accademia Bridge and soak in the fabulous views. Now walk back the way you came. Go past bridges 16, 17, 18 and 19 on your left. Soon you will arrive at bridge 15. Cross this bridge. Go straight and you will discover bridge 21.

Now you have a fairly long walk to bridge 22. First, cross bridge 21 and go until the street dead ends. Turn right just under the wood beams. Walk straight until the street dead ends. Turn left at the sign "Crosera". Now take the first street on the right, Ramo Di Piscina. Continue on this street. Soon it veers to the left. Up ahead you will see bridge 22.

Cross bridge 22 and bridge 23 will be on your right. Leave bridge 23 on your right as you continue straight along side the canal. You will then be forced to turn left. Walk a few steps and turn left again. Now after a few steps turn right at the well head and walk straight and you will come to the Grand Canal again and to Sant Ángelo vaporetto stop. This completes Bridge Tour 1. This location is also the starting point of Bridge Tour 2.

This tour contains 17 bridges. It starts at the Sant Ángelo vaporetto stop and ends at St. Mark's Square. Leave the vaporetto and walk straight to the Corte De L' Albero sign. Turn left at this sign. Then turn right and you will see bridge 24. Cross it and go straight and you will come to bridge 25. Do not cross this bridge. Turn around and take a few steps. Then take the first left. As you get into Campo S. Angelo, a large courtyard, stay near the church on your right. Notice the leaning tower visible from the courtyard. Look to the right and you will see bridge 26. When you get to this bridge, walk to the left along the canal. Then you will be at bridge 27. Do not cross bridge 27.

Look to the left and go to the narrow street named Calle Caotorta. Take this street and it will lead you to bridge 28, Ponte Storto. As you cross bridge 28 turn left and go across bridge 29. Turn left and then right. Now go straight to a courtyard with a church in the center. On the right is the famous La Fenice theatre. The most famous opera house in Venice, La Fenice (The Phoenix), was completed in 1792. This building replaced an older theatre that had been consumed by fire. La Fenice was a glorious symbol of Venice. In 1836 this opera house burned to the ground. La Fenice was rebuilt and prospered until 1996 when fire once again consumed it. The theatre has been rebuilt and it opened in 2003. There are several nice restaurants in the courtyard, however they are rather expensive.

Take the first left in the courtyard and walk to bridge 30, Ponte De La Verona. This bridge was constructed in 1864. Walk straight to Calle De La Mandola. Continue straight and you will come to bridge 31, Ponte De La Cortesia. Cross this bridge.

Walk left to bridge 32, Ponte De S. Paternian. Do not cross this bridge. Walk through the courtyard, staying to the left. Take the first left turn and then another left. Walk behind the church. There you will find bridge 33. Now retrace your steps back to bridge 31.

With bridge 31 to your back, walk straight. Turn right at the statue. Walk straight. When the street comes to an end turn right. Bridge 34 is ahead. Cross this bridge. Walk straight until you must make a turn. Turn right and you will come to bridge 35.

Cross bridge 35 and you will re-enter the courtyard at La Fenice. Walk to the left, around the church. Continue to the back of the church. Just a little beyond the church you will find bridge 36.

Cross bridge 36 and walk straight as far as you can. Now make a mandatory left turn. Take the next right, then the next left. Bridge 37 will appear.

At bridge 37 you will find a wonderful "Self Service" restaurant. The menu is in English. The food is good and the prices are reasonable. Beside this restaurant is a fabulous Venetian glass shop. Cross bridge 37. Walk until you are forced to make a turn. Turn right and soon you will be at bridge 38. To the left is bridge 39, a new wood bridge. Beyond this bridge you can see bridge 40. Cross bridge 38 and walk along the left side, staying under the Porticos (arches). You are now in the famous St. Mark's Square. Take the first main street on the left and you will find bridge 40, Ponte Dei Dai. This is the end of Tour 2. St. Mark's Square is also the starting point of Tour 3.

Railing on bridge 30

This tour contains 18 bridges. It starts and ends at St. Mark's Square.   Place yourself on the north side of the square. If you are standing in front of St. Mark's Basilica with your back toward it, the north side is on your right. Look for a street named Sotoportego Dei Dai. As you turn onto this street you will see bridge 40, Ponte Dei Dai. Cross bridge 40 and take the first left, then the first right. Now walk a short distance and take the first right and walk straight until you encounter bridge 41.

Cross bridge 41 and take the first left. Soon you will discover bridge 42. Cross this bridge. Now turn left and then turn right when you are forced to do so. Next turn left on the first street you come to. After a very brief stroll you will be at bridge 43, Ponte De Le Balote. Cross it and then take the first left. Bridge 44 will soon appear. Instead of crossing it, turn around and head back the way you came by continuing straight to the fourth street on the right from bridge 44. Make a right turn here onto Calle Del Teatro O Del La Commedia. Bridge 45 is just ahead. There is a good Gelato shop at this bridge.

Do not cross bridge 45. Turn around and take the first street to the right. This will take you to the Grand Canal. Once there turn right and bridge 46 is ahead. Cross this bridge and continue walking along the Grand Canal to the first street on the right, Calle larga Mazzini. Continue straight and then just before reaching the next canal, veer slightly to the right onto Calle de Le Acque. Bridge 47 is ahead. Instead of crossing it, turn right and walk along the canal. Bridge 48, Ponte Dei Bareteri, soon appears. Bridge 49 is on the right.

Cross bridge 48. You will be on the famous shopping street called the Merceria between St. Mark's Square and the Rialto Bridge. After walking for about 100 meters, you will notice a short alley to the left that leads around a church. Walk around the left side of this church. Upon arriving at the rear of this church, turn left and then right on the second street. This leads to bridge 50, Ponte De La Malvasia.

Once at bridge 50 turn around and go back to the first street you encounter and turn left. After a short distance veer left. Straight ahead you will find bridge 51, Ponte Balbi. Once again turn around and go back the way you came. Take the first left and then take another left. This leads to bridge 52 on the left.

Cross bridge 52 and turn right at the first opportunity. Now take the only street to the right before you reach a dead end at a canal. Turn left after a very short walk. This will take you along side a canal that leads to bridge 53. Just after you cross bridge 53, turn left to reach bridge 54.

At bridge 54 turn around and head back the way you came. Take the first left and then turn left again at the first opportunity. As you reach bridge 55, locate bridge 54 on your left and four other bridges on your right. The first bridge on the right is bridge 56. To get there, turn around and turn left at the first opportunity. Then turn left again and bridge 56 will appear.

Don't cross bridge 56, just stroll along side the canal and bridge 57 is on your left. Walk to the middle of this bridge. Notice the bridges on both sides. This location gives you another view of the Bridge of Sighs. Bridge 57 is the last bridge of Tour 3. To get back to St. Mark's Square, walk back toward bridge 56. When you reach it, turn left and proceed straight until you enter St. Mark's Square. This marks the end of Tour 3. Café Florian is located on the south side of St. Mark's Square.

Railing on bridge 42

This tour consists of 19 bridges. It starts at the group of San Zaccaria vaporetto stops and ends at the famous Rialto Bridge. At the start there are four or five vaporetto stops in a group, all are named San Zaccaria. Find the first bridge in this tour by locating the large statue in the middle of the walkway by the water. The first bridge on the left of this statue is bridge 58U, named Ponte del Vin. It is beside the Hotel Danieli. The reason for the unusual number of the bridge was at the time I developed this tour it was unavailable to photograph because of barriers and scaffolding. This is the first bridge of the tour.

On the left side of bridge 58U is a street named Calle De Le Rasse. Take this street. Walk until the street comes to an end. Turn right and you will see bridge 58. Cross bridge 58 and take the first left. Soon you will arrive at bridge 59 on your left. Cross bridge 59 and wind your way until the street ends. Turn left. This leads to bridge 60. Cross it and take the first right, then the second right. Now you will be at bridge 61. Don't cross it, instead take the first right and then a right in the courtyard at the address 4395B. You will come to bridge 62 on your right and then bridge 63 also on your right. Then you will encounter a small, private bridge. Continue straight and bridge 64 will appear.

Cross bridge 64. Bridge 65 is on the right and bridge 66 is on your left. Do not cross bridge 65 or bridge 66. Ahead is the large, well known church Santa Maria Formosa. The current building was constructed in 1492. Walk around the church and you will soon see four more bridges, all on the right. They are numbers 67, 68, 69 and 70 respectively.

When you get to bridge 70 do not cross it. Instead walk all the way around the church, as far as you can go. Then you will encounter bridge 71 on the left. Do not cross this bridge. You will see bridge 72 on the right.

Cross bridge 72. Go about 100 meters and turn right onto Salizada S. Lio, a busy street. Walk straight until you see the sign "Calle De La Fava" as a small courtyard appears. Turn left onto this Calle. Walk to the end of the street and turn right. Follow this street to bridge 73. Do not cross bridge 73. Go back around the left side of the church. Then take the first left turn. When you get back to the small courtyard, turn left. Bridge 74 is just ahead.

Cross bridge 74. Look on the left wall of the building and notice the sign that reads "Per Rialto" with an arrow under it. Now follow these signs and the groups of people until you arrive at bridge 75, the most famous bridge in Venice. It is named Ponte del Rialto (the Rialto Bridge). This tour ends here. The Rialto Bridge is also the start of Tour 5.

Rialto Bridge

This tour is comprised of 20 bridges. The tour starts at the Rialto Bridge and ends at the San Zaccaria Monumento vaporetto stop. Included in this tour is a stop in the small courtyard where Marco Polo's house once stood.

Start at the southeast side (the side toward St. Mark's Square) of the Rialto Bridge. Facing the bridge and standing on the third step, walk to your right and then onto Calle Del Fontego Dei Tedeschi. Take the first left. Cross bridge 76. Turn right as you reach the San Giovanni Crisostomo church. Marco Polo's home once stood on the perimeter of the courtyard surrounding the church. Stop in this courtyard and think of how life must have been 744 years ago as young Marco, then ten years old, played in the courtyard and ran over the nearby bridges. Now take the second right. This street becomes Calle del Miliòn. This street takes you to bridge 77. Notice the name of this bridge, Ponte Marco Polo.

Walk to the center of bridge 77 and stop. As you gaze out over the canal, place in your mind the vision of young Marco Polo, over seven centuries ago, also gazing out over the water, dreaming of someday voyaging far, far away. His travels took him all the way to China! The dreams of a young boy were realized. Now cross this bridge. Then take the first right at the end of the street. Now turn left. Go about 3 feet. Now turn right. Bridge 78 is ahead. Cross bridge 78 and you will arrive at San Lio church and the wide street Salizada S. Lio (yes you have been here before if you have taken Tour 4). Walk all the way around the church. Take the first street on the left. Calle De Le Vele. This leads to bridge 79.

Once you are at bridge 79, you will see bridges 80 and 81 on your right. Walk back out to Salizada S. Lio Street. Turn left on it. Then take the first left and go to bridge 80. Now again go back to Salizada S. Lio and turn left and then left again to get to bridge 81. Upon reaching bridge 81, once again go back out to Salizada S. Lio Street and turn left.

Now walk along Salizada S. Lio Street and take the second left onto Calle del Paradiso. This street leads to bridge 82. Bridge 83 is a few feet to the right. Cross bridge 82 and turn left. At the first opportunity to turn left, do so again. Just a few steps will get you to bridge 84. Don't cross this bridge. Turn around and walk straight until you reach bridge 85.

Cross bridge 85 and soon you will enter the large courtyard Campo Santa Maria Formosa with the church in front of you. As you walk toward the church, take the first left at address 6130. Shortly you will arrive at a bridge not numbered or photographed. As you stand at the bridge, look to your left. You will see bridge 86. Walk to it but don't cross it. Turn around and cross the bridge not numbered. This street is Calle De Le Modoneta.

Stay on Calle De Le Modoneta until it forces you to turn either left or right. Turn left. Take the next left and arrive at bridge 87. Do not cross bridge 87. Turn around. Take the first left. When you reach the canal, keep walking and you will see bridge 88. Don't cross this bridge either. Turn around and take the first left, which is named Borgoloco S. Lorenzo. This street takes you to bridge 89. Do not cross bridge 89. Just walk past it along the canal. You can see bridge 90 as you approach it.

When you get to bridge 90 don't cross it. Continue walking along the canal and take the first opportunity to turn left (onto Calle Dei Preti). After a short walk, you will be at another canal. To your left you will see bridge 91. To your right is bridge 92. Go toward bridge 92. As you get near it, bridge 93 is directly ahead. Do not cross either bridge. Instead, turn right and leave bridge 93 on your left. As you walk along another canal, you will come to bridge 94.

Cross bridge 94. Turn right. You will see another bridge (from Tour 4) on your right. Continue past it and then take the next left. Now continue on this somewhat winding street. Turn left at address 4700, then walk to the right and you will see an archway. Beyond that is the huge body of water named the Canal of San Marco. When you arrive at the water, turn left and go past the statue. After a brief walk you will be at bridge 95. End the tour by going to the nearby vaporetto stop, San Zaccaria Monumento. This is also the starting point for Tour 6.

Tour 6, Bridges 96 – 114

This tour consists of 19 bridges. It begins at San Zaccaria Monumento vaporetto stop and ends at Arsenale vaporetto stop. This vaporetto location is next to bridge 95. Leave the vaporetto and cross this bridge. The next bridge is bridge 96. After seeing it, turn around and go back toward bridge 95.

Between bridges 95 and 96 is the La Pietà church. This is the church where Antonio Vivaldi spent almost 4 decades of his life. La Pietà is where he composed nearly all his concertos. Beside the church is Calle della Pietà. Take this street and turn at the next right. This leads you to bridge 97. Cross this bridge and then walk on the left side of the courtyard until you see the street Salizada S. Antonin. This will be the third street on the left. Turn here and soon bridge 98 will appear. Don't cross it, just walk along side the canal and you will arrive at bridge 99.

Cross bridge 99 and walk along side the canal on your right. This stroll leads you to bridge 100. Cross it and take the first left. When forced to turn, turn left and then right. Walk to bridge 101 and cross it. On the left you will see bridge 102. On the right you will see bridge 172 from Tour 10.

To get to bridge 103, go back over bridge 101 and then turn left. After a short walk, turn left on Ramo Al Ponte S. Francesco. This street will lead to bridge 103. To get to bridge 104 requires a fair amount of winding through several streets.

Do not cross bridge 103. Start with bridge 103 to your back. Walk straight until you are forced to make a turn. Turn left. Then immediately turn left again on Calle De L' Ogio. Walk straight and take the last left turn, which will be onto Ramo Baffo. Now you will arrive in a small courtyard. On the left side of the courtyard is bridge 104. On the right side is bridge 105. Cross bridge 105. Turn right at the first opportunity. This will place you on the street named Calle Magno. You will go through a small courtyard named Campo Do Pozzi. At the end of the street turn right at address 2667A.

Bridge 106 is just ahead. Do not cross bridge 106. Turn around and go to the second street on the right. Turn to the right here and you will see bridge 107. Don't cross this bridge. Instead, turn around and take the first right turn. In just a few steps, the street turns to the right. Continue on and wind around, staying to the right. Soon you will discover bridge 108.

Cross bridge 108 and take the first left turn. Now take the second left turn which leads to a canal. Walk along side the canal and you will come to bridge 109. Cross it and just a short distance ahead you will see bridge 110 on the left. Do not cross this bridge. Walk past bridge 110, keeping it on your left. Continue walking along side the canal and you will arrive at bridge 111 and then 112. Do not cross these two bridges.

Turn around and return to bridge 110. Do not cross this bridge. Take the first left past bridge 110 and you will discover bridge 113, however do not cross it. Walk along side the canal. Leave the canal by turning left. Then take the first right. Now walk straight and you will arrive at the large body of water named Canal of San Marco. On your right will be bridge 114. This bridge is named Ponte Della Ca" Di Dio. This ends Tour 6. The Arsenale vaporetto stop is in front of you.

Vivaldi plaque on La Pietà church between bridges 95 & 96

Tour 7, Bridges 115 – 126

This tour is composed of 12 bridges. The tour starts at the Arsenale vaporetto stop and finishes at the Giardini vaporetto stop. Upon exiting the vaporetto, turn right and walk along the canal until you arrive at bridge 115. Cross this bridge and continue along the canal to bridge 116. Now turn around and head back to bridge 115. Turn right just before stepping onto bridge 115.

Walk along side the small canal and you will see bridge 117 ahead. When you get to this bridge, look ahead and you will see bridge 118. Centuries ago the twin towers at this gate marked the entrance to the Arsenale. This was the shipyard of Venice for centuries and is still off limits to visitors. Thousands of ships claimed the Arsenale their home port during Venice's period of world trade.

From bridge 117, turn around and walk back with the canal on your right. Take the first left onto Campo De La Tana. This street will lead to bridge 119. Cross this bridge and turn left, walking along side the canal for a nice long stroll. Take the last right turn (onto Calle Bassa) before the street ends. Now take the first left and you will see bridge 120.

Cross bridge 120 and just ahead you will see bridge 121. Instead of crossing this bridge, turn left at it. Walk until you reach a small canal. Turn left and discover bridge 122. Cross this bridge and take the second left onto Calle Ruga. Walk straight ahead and just before the street ends at a canal, turn left onto Ramo S. Daniel and you will see bridge 123. This bridge is gated and you cannot cross it.

From bridge 123, turn around and take the first right. Walk straight and soon you will pass through a small courtyard named Campo Ruga. Then continue straight on Calle Ruga. Soon you will arrive at bridge 124. Cross this bridge and then bridge 125 will appear on your left.

Do not cross bridge 125, instead turn right along side the canal. You will pass bridge 121 on your right. Continue into the wide boulevard street ahead. Enter the large park on the left. Walk past the statue of Garibaldi. You will cross bridge 127 in Tour 8.

Now you will be at the large Canal of San Marco. Bridge 126 is on the right. The Giardini vaporetto stop is in front of you. This is the end of Tour 7.

Railing on bridge 126

Tour 8, Bridges 127 – 134

This tour contains 8 bridges. The tour begins at the Giardini vaporetto stop and finishes at the Sant' Élena vaporetto stop. After leaving the vaporetto stop, walk away from the water. Directly on your left by the water is bridge 126. Walk straight ahead and veer to the left. This takes you to bridge 127. Do not cross this bridge. Turn around and take the first left into a large park. Go past a narrow path on the right. Continue ahead and you will be forced to turn either left or right. Turn right onto the wider street. Then take the first left. Now make another left turn. This will lead to bridge 128.

Cross bridge 128 and immediately turn right and walk along side the canal. Bridge 129 is just ahead. Don't cross bridge 129. Continue walking along side the canal and soon bridge 130 will appear. Cross this bridge. Turn right and walk until the street ends. Now turn right again. Almost immediately turn left and then left again. This street goes to a canal and then turns right. Now you see bridge 131 ahead.

Don't cross bridge 131, instead turn around and start back the way you came. You will leave the canal as the street makes a left turn. Go to near the end of this street and turn right on Ramo Secondo Del Paludo. Now take a left turn. Walk straight through the archway and back into the park. Find your way back to the water's edge and turn left. Walk along the water's edge and follow it as it curves left. Bridge 133 will appear. Cross this bridge. From here you can see bridge 132, but it is difficult to get to the bridge. It's not worth the effort! Now walk along the water's edge to the Sant' Elena vaporetto stop.

This is probably where you will desire to end the tour. There are four more bridges beyond this vaporetto stop. They are a long walk from here, and are not at all spectacular. However, if you wish to see them, continue walking past this vaporetto stop, staying along the water's edge. When you are forced to turn left, walk a short distance and bridge 134 will be on your right. The three remaining bridges will be in a row crossing the canal on your right. These bridges are spaced far apart. If you do visit these bridges, you will need to retrace your steps and return to the Sant' Élena vaporetto stop.

Railing on bridge 145

Scuola Grande di San Marco near bridge 156

Tour 9 includes 19 bridges. The tour starts at the Cá d' Oro vaporetto stop and ends at the Fondamenta Nove vaporetto stop. As you exit the vaporetto, walk straight on Calle delle Cá d' Oro. Take the first left and bridge 135 is ahead. If you just can't resist those golden arches, you can visit the McDonald's restaurant in this area. However, for more local delicacies you can step into one of the three bakeries also nearby.

Cross bridge 135 and walk along side the canal to bridge 136. Do not cross this bridge. Continue walking straight and bridge 138 will appear. Just beyond it is bridge 139. Cross bridge 138 and take the first right. Bridge 137 is just a few steps away. Do not cross bridge 137.

Turn around and walk straight. Bridge 140 is not far ahead. Cross it and turn right. You will see bridge 141 ahead. Cross it and walk straight to bridge 142. Do not cross this bridge. Turn right and walk along side the canal to reach bridge 143. Cross number 143 and walk straight to bridge 144.

Do not cross bridge 144. Ahead you will see bridge 145. Cross it and take the left fork in the alleyway. This will end at a wide street called Strada Nova. Turn left onto this street. Continue straight and you will arrive at bridge 146 on the right. Cross this bridge and turn left, then right. Wind through two small courtyards and you will see bridge 147. Don't cross this bridge. Stand facing bridge 147. Now turn left and walk on the street named Salizada S. Canzian. When you get to an open area, in front of you is the sign "Campiello Bruno Crovato Gia S. Canzian". Turn left here.

Bridge 148 comes into view. No photograph was taken of this bridge. Cross it and take the first right onto Sotoportego De La Cason. Now take the first left. Next take the second right onto Rio Terà SS. Apostoli. Now take the second right onto Rio Terà Barba Frutariol and walk straight to bridge 149. Don't cross this bridge. Turn around and take the second opportunity to turn right. This will lead to bridge 150.

Cross bridge 150 and take the first right to get to bridge 151. Don't cross number 151. Turn around and take the first right. Bridge 152 is just ahead. Cross it and walk straight to the water. You will walk past the magnificent Chiesa dei Gesuiti Baroque church. This church houses many paintings, including some masterpieces by Tintoretto and Titian.

Turn right at the water's edge and bridge 153 will be a short walk. This is the last bridge on this tour. Beside this bridge is the group of Fondamenta Nove vaporetto stops. The Alguibario café and snack bar is located here. It has good sandwiches and drinks for reasonable prices. This is the end of tour 9.

Railing on bridge 165

Tour 10, Bridges 154 – 172

This tour is composed of 19 bridges. It begins at the Fondamenta Nove vaporetto stop and ends at the Ospedale vaporetto stop. As you leave the vaporetto turn left and stroll along the water's edge. The first bridge you come to will be number 154, Ponte Panada. Cross it and a little further on will be bridge 155, Ponte Dei Mendicanti. Just after you cross bridge 155 turn right and walk along side the canal.

After a fairly long stroll along the water's edge you will reach bridge 156. On the left is the large, beautiful church of Giovanni Paolo. Construction on this outstanding Gothic structure began in 1246. Giovanni Paolo church is filled with extraordinary sculptures. Cross this bridge and soon you will be at number 157. Cross this one as well and then you will encounter bridge 158. After you cross number 158, bridge 159 is just a few steps away. As you stand facing bridge 159, do not cross it. Turn around and take the first street on your right, Calle Larga Widmann. Now you will cross bridge 160 and continue walking straight.

Walk all the way around the building on your left. Then you will discover bridge 162. Cross it and take a left and then another left. Here is bridge 161. Turn around here and walk straight. When you reach a very small courtyard named Campiello Crosetta, turn left. Ahead of you is a large church and bridge 159 again. Cross this bridge and go right. Now on the right will be bridge 163. Do not cross this bridge. With bridge 163 to your back, walk away from it and take the first right.

Keep winding around on this street and you will come to a small canal and three bridges. Pass by the first bridge which was being repaired and was not photographed. Now arrive at bridge 164 on your left. Now cross bridge 165 which is straight ahead. Now you will enter Campo S. Marina. Stay on the left side of this courtyard. Take the first left turn. You will cross bridges 84 and 85 from another tour.

Enter Campo S. Maria Formosa. Halfway down on the left will be Calle Longa S. Maria Formosa. Turn onto this street. Now walk until you see address 6206. Turn left at the street just beyond this address. The name of this street is Calle Trevisana O Cicogna. Walk straight and you will come to bridge 166. Cross it and turn right. Now you will come to bridge 167. Do not cross this bridge. Turn around and then make a right turn. Walk straight and then turn right at the church. Now turn right at address 6362 onto Calle De L' Ospealeto. This leads to bridge 168.

Cross bridge 168 and turn left. Up ahead you will see bridge 169. Do not cross this bridge. With bridge 169 on your left, turn right onto a short street. Follow the sharp turn to the left by a small canal. Now make a left turn onto another street named Ramo Cappello (On the right is bridge 87 included in Tour 5). After making this left turn onto Ramo Cappello, bridge 170 is just ahead.

Cross bridge 170 and turn left when the street ends. Now immediately turn right. When this street ends, turn right. Continue straight until the street you are on empties into a small courtyard. Go to the street in the far right corner of the courtyard. The street is named Calle Zon. This street will lead to bridge 171.

As you cross bridge 171 you will see number 172 on your right. You can walk to it but do not cross it. This is the last bridge in this tour. Go back across bridge 171. Enter the courtyard you were just in. Walk to the far right corner of the courtyard and turn right onto Calle de Le Capucine. When you reach the water's edge, turn left. Ahead is the Ospedale vaporetto stop. This is the end of Tour 10.

Tour 11, Bridges 173 – 187

This tour consists of 15 bridges. The tour begins at the Tre Archi vaporetto stop and ends at the Sant' Alvise vaporetto stop. As you leave the vaporetto, turn right and walk along side the canal and you will see bridge 173 ahead. This bridge is named Ponte dei Tre Archi. Do not cross this bridge. Continue walking along side the canal until you come to the third turn to the left at address 1038. This street is named Sotoportego Dei Vedei. This street will lead you to bridge 174.

Do not cross bridge 174. Turn around and go back to the canal you started at. Turn left and walk along side the canal again and then take the second left. This street, Calle De Le Chioverette, goes straight to bridge 175. Do not cross this bridge. Turn around and again go back to the canal you started at. Turn left and continue walking along side the canal until you come to bridge 176. This is a wide bridge. Do not cross this bridge. Turn around and walk back in the direction you came. Go to the third right turn past the bridge. You will be near address 1249. Turn right here.

You are now in the Ghetto area of Venice. This location is generally recognized as the oldest Jewish ghetto in the world. As you continue on this street you will pass a Jewish synagogue on your right. Bridge 177 is just ahead. Cross it and you will enter the large ghetto courtyard. This courtyard has three well-heads in it. Turn right in the courtyard and walk on Sotoportego De Gheto Novo Street. Now you will see bridge 178. Do not cross it, instead turn around and walk back to the courtyard. Bridge 179 is on your right at the end of the courtyard. You may notice that bridge 178 and bridge 179 have the same name. In Venice this does occur occasionally.

Cross bridge 179 and turn left. Soon you will be at bridges 180 and 181. Cross bridge 180 and now bridge 181 is on the left. Cross bridge 181, turn to the right and walk along side the canal. Next you will come to bridge 182. Cross it and turn left. After a fairly long walk you will discover bridge 183 straight ahead. Cross it and immediately turn left. Bridge 184 is just a short walk along the canal.

To get to bridge 185 you need to go back to bridge 182. To accomplish this, start at bridge 184. Walk with the canal on your right. Now cross back over bridge 183. The next bridge you see will be bridge 182. Do not cross bridge 182. Take the first left turn after the bridge. This street goes directly to bridge 185. Do not cross this bridge.

Turn around and go back to the canal you were just at. Turn left at the canal. You will go past bridge 181 on the right then you will cross bridge 180. Immediately turn left onto Calle Turlona. Bridge 186 crosses the next canal ahead. As you cross this bridge turn left and then right. You will soon arrive at bridge 187. This marks the last bridge on this tour.

At this point you have two options. First, you can easily get into Tour 12. To do this, simply turn right immediately after crossing bridge 187. As you walk along the canal you will see bridge 188, the starting point of Tour 12. Second, if you desire to end your bridge sightings for the day, follow these directions. After turning right at bridge 187, take the first street to the left. Just before this street ends turn right onto Ramo Novo De La Rotonda. Take the first left. You will arrive at the Sant' Alvise vaporetto stop.

Railing on bridge 179

Tour 12, Bridges 188 – 201

This tour contains 14 bridges. The tour starts at the Sant' Alvise vaporetto stop and is completed at the Madonna dell' Orto vaporetto stop. Exiting the vaporetto, take the first left. You will then have to turn right. Continue walking primarily straight and you will come upon bridge 188. Cross it and continue on to bridge 189. Cross this bridge. Continue straight again and you will discover bridge 190. Just before you would cross this bridge, turn to the left and walk along side the canal to reach bridge 191.

Do not cross bridge 191. Continue walking in the same direction along side the canal. Bridge 192 will be on your right and straight ahead is bridge 193. Cross number 193 and then you will see bridge 194 ahead. Do not cross bridge 194. Turn around and go back across number 193. Take the second street to the right after bridge 193. This will lead you to bridge 195. Just before bridge 195 is a small, quaint bakery. Cross this bridge and immediately turn left. There you will discover bridge 196. Do not cross this bridge.

At bridge 196 turn around and go back past bridge 195. (Another bridge is in the area but was under renovation and not accessible during the writing of this book). Bridge 197 is just a short walk straight ahead.

Cross bridge 197. Bridge 198 will be on your right. Walk past number 198 without crossing it. The street will leave the canal by turning left. After you do this, take the first right turn. Now you will come upon bridge 199. Cross this bridge and you will see bridge 215 found in Tour 13. At bridge 215, turn left and bridge 200 will soon appear. Cross it and turn left, walking along side the canal.

After a leisurely stroll you will encounter bridge 201, the last one on this tour. To end the tour, walk past this bridge without crossing it. Then take the first street on the right, Calle Larga Piave. It will make a right turn and then veer to the right. Now follow the vaporetto signs. Soon you will be at the Madonna dell' Orto vaporetto stop. This ends Tour 12.

View of Santa Maria della Salute from under the Accademia Bridge

Santa Maria della Salute church

This tour is composed of 16 bridges. The tour begins at the San Marcuola vaporetto stop that is nearest the right side of the church and ends at the Ca' d' Oro vaporetto stop. Leave the vaporetto and walk away from the water, staying to your right. Take the first right and you will cross bridge 202. Immediately turn left along side the canal.

As the street ends along the canal, it will cause you to turn right. Then take the first left. After a brief walk turn left and you will see bridge 203. Do not cross it. Turn around and walk on the wide street named Rio terrà della Maddalena. After passing five streets on your right you will enter an open area. Straight ahead will be bridge 210 (discussed later in this tour) and on the right will be bridge 204.

Walk past bridge 204 staying along side the canal. Next will be bridge 205. Do not cross it. Walk to the right and then take the first left onto Calle de L' Ogio. Veer to the left. Now you will cross bridge 206 and then immediately turn left and walk along side the canal. When the street ends turn right and you will arrive at bridge 207. Do not cross bridge 207.

With bridge 207 to your back, walk straight ahead and then take the first right just before you reach the church. Bridge 208 will soon appear. Cross this bridge and walk to number 209 just ahead. Cross this bridge and you will see bridge 210 on the right. Now go back across bridge 209 and turn left. Bridge 211 is straight ahead. Cross it and turn right along side the canal. Follow this canal. Bridge 212 will be on your right. Cross this bridge and you will see bridge 213.

Instead of crossing bridge 213 turn left and you will discover bridge 214 just beyond the church. After crossing bridge 214 resist the temptation to go straight ahead to a large bridge. This is bridge 217 and you will soon visit it. Instead, just after crossing bridge 214 turn right and then take the first left. Walk straight to bridge 215. Cross this bridge and turn right. After a nice stroll along side the canal you will arrive at bridge 216.

Cross bridge 216 and walk straight, traveling along side another canal on your left. Bridge 217 will soon come into view. This is the last bridge on this tour. Cross it and turn right. You will be walking along side a canal and soon come upon several bridges (numbers 139, 138, 136 and then 135) from Tour 9. There is a church between bridges 136 and 135. Cross bridge 135 just beyond the church. The smell of home made cosmetics will beckon you into the local shop on the left just past the bridge.

A little further down the street three bakeries on the left and right will provide additional delight to your senses of smell and sight! And then, as in several other tours, the American institution McDonald's restaurant will appear. Go to the next street and turn right. This street is named Calle Ca' d' Oro. At the end of this short street you will come to the Grand Canal and the Ca' d' Oro vaporetto stop.

This area is also the location of the once glorious Ca' d' Oro palace. In 1420 conversion began on the building located at the site. The result of this work was a palace given the name "House of Gold", Ca' d' Oro. The façade was initially covered with gold, however centuries of weather have removed this gilding. This is the end of Tour 13 and also the start of Tour 14.

Railing on bridge 203

Tour 14, Bridges 218 – 224

You will visit 7 bridges on this tour. The start of the tour is at the Tre Archi vaporetto stop and the end is at the Ferrovia degli Scalzi vaporetto stop. Exit the vaporetto and turn right. Walk along side the canal and you will soon arrive at bridge 173 found in Tour 11. Cross this bridge. On your right you will see bridge 218. Do not cross this bridge.

With bridge 173 to your back, walk straight ahead and soon a church will appear on the left and a canal on the right. Ahead of you will be an iron gate that is probably open. Walk through the gate and you will see bridge 219. At the other side of this wood bridge is a locked gate. Walk to the middle of this bridge and you can see bridge 222 to your left.

Now turn around and go back through the open gate. Return to the large canal at bridge 173. Turn right at the canal. Walk past the Crea vaporetto stop. Here is bridge 220. Don't cross this bridge. Turn right and there is a new wood bridge across the small canal. This is bridge 221. Now go back to the large canal and turn right. The 5th street on the right is Calle del Camin. Take this street and walk straight. After a while you will see the sign for Calle della Misericordia. Do not turn here. Continue straight ahead and shortly you will need to veer to the right.

Soon you will see bridge 223. Do not cross it. Turn around and go straight. After a short walk you will come to the Grand Canal. Bridge 224, Ponte degli Scalzi is on the right. This is the last bridge on Tour 14. To end the tour do not cross this bridge, instead go to the vaporetto stop located to the right of the bridge. This is the Ferrovia degli Scalzi stop.

Bridge 224, Ponte degli Scalzi

Railing on bridge 227

Tour 15, Bridges 225 – 233

This tour consists of 9 bridges. This tour begins at the Piazzale Roma vaporetto stop and finishes at this same vaporetto stop. Exit the vaporetto and turn left. You will reach bridge 301 from another tour. Turn right before the bridge and walk along side the small canal. Walk past the bridge on your left, number 298 from another tour. Next you will cross another bridge. This bridge was not photographed or numbered.

After you cross this bridge you will arrive at another canal just ahead. Look above the entrance to the canal street. The street you want to take has two signs. They are "Sotoportego De Ca' Bernardo" and "Fondamenta De Ca' Bernardo". Turn right and walk with the canal on your left. After a short stroll you will arrive at bridge 225.

Do not cross bridge 225. Walk a little further and turn left. Now turn right onto a wide street. Go to the water's edge and turn left. Bridge 226 is on the right. Do not cross it. Walk past it and turn to the left as another canal appears. Now you will see bridge 227 on your right. Leave this bridge on your right and walk past it. Soon you will cross bridge 228. Then bridge 229 will appear.

Cross bridge 229 and bridge 230 will be on your left. Do not cross bridge 230. Go back across number 229 and continue walking straight. Shortly you will cross bridge 231 and then number 232 will be on your right. Do not cross bridge 232. Continue walking straight and soon bridge 233 will appear on your right.

Now you will once again cross the bridge that was not photographed or numbered. You can end the tour by crossing this bridge and walking straight until you come to the Grand Canal. Bridge 301 (from Tour 19) will be on the right. Do not cross this bridge. Turn left at the bridge and walk along side the Grand Canal until you come to the first vaporetto stop. This stop, named Piazzale Roma, marks the end of Tour 15.

As an alternative you may desire to start directly into Tour 16 by crossing bridge 233 and then turning right to get to bridge 234, the initial bridge in Tour 16.

Example of Canal and Bridge Maintenance

Tour 16, Bridges 234 – 252

This tour contains 19 bridges. The tour starts at the Piazzale Roma vaporetto stop and ends at the San Basílio vaporetto stop. Upon exiting the vaporetto turn left. Walk a short distance along side the Grand Canal. The first bridge you encounter will be number 301 from Tour 19. Do not cross this bridge. Turn right at the bridge and walk along side the small canal on your left. You will pass bridge 298 (from Tour 19) on your left.

Soon you will begin to cross a bridge from Tour 15. When you are on top of this bridge, turn left and cross bridge 233 also from Tour 15. Now turn right and bridge 234 is just ahead. Cross this bridge. On your right is bridge 232 from Tour 15. Turn left and you will see bridge 235 up ahead. Do not cross this bridge. At the bridge turn right.

When this street ends bridge 236 will be on the right. Cross this bridge and turn left. The next bridge you see will be number 237. Do not cross it. Now stroll past bridges 238, 239 and 240 without crossing any of them. When you get to bridge 241, turn right without crossing it as well.

As you leave bridge 241 you will see bridge 242 ahead and on the left. Straight ahead is bridge 222 from another tour. Cross number 242 and after a short walk you will arrive at bridge 243. Do not cross number 243. Continue walking along side the canal on your right and you will discover bridge 244. Cross it and walk straight along side the canal to bridge 245. Cross this bridge and turn right. Walk along side the canal and you will encounter bridge 246. Do not cross this bridge.

After leaving bridge 246 on your right, walk straight a very short distance and then briefly wind around, staying to your right, until another canal appears on your right. Now walk along side this canal and bridge 247 will soon appear. Do not cross it. Continue walking by the canal and up ahead you will see number 248.

Cross bridge 248 and immediately turn left along the canal. Take the first street to the left, Calle De La Madalena. This street leads to number 249. Cross this bridge and turn right. Continue walking along the canal, passing bridges 250 and 251 on your right. Do not cross either one of these bridges. After passing bridge 251 follow the street by staying to the right. When you arrive at the water's edge bridge 252 will be on the right. Beside you will be the vaporetto stop San Basílio which is the end of this tour.

Railing on bridge 235

Railing on bridge 236

Tour 17, Bridges 253 – 267

This tour includes 15 bridges. The tour begins at the Salute vaporetto stop and ends at the Záttere Ponte Lungo vaporetto stop. Step off the vaporetto and Santa Maria della Salute is in front of you. This magnificent church has numerous treasures to behold. Paintings by Tintoretto and Titian, as well as many other famous painters, can be found inside. More detailed information about Santa Maria della Salute can be found in the History section of this book.

Walk straight a very short distance to arrive at bridge 253. Do not cross it but continue walking to bridge 254. Do not cross this bridge either. Continue walking and now bridge 255 appears. Cross this bridge and then turn left. Walk straight to the water's edge. Bridge 256 is on your left.

Instead of crossing bridge 256, turn right and walk along the water's edge. After a pleasant stroll you will arrive at number 257. Turn right just before entering this bridge. Walk along side the small canal to bridge 258. Do not cross this bridge.

For a quick side tour, turn right at the first street beyond bridge 258. About half way down this short street, find the plaque above a door on the right side. Notice the name of Ezra Pound, a famous American poet of the 20th century. Pound lived in this house at various times during his life, especially in his later years.

Ezra Pound was a controversial poet during his time however he is considered one of the great poets of the 20th century. Pound loved Venice, as evidenced by the portion of his poem "Night Litany" presented at the beginning of this book. He is buried in Venice on San Michele Island. This house in Venice is currently owned by Pound's daughter, Mary de Rachewiltz.

Mary lives in an 11th century castle in the Italian Alps. She is a most gracious and intelligent lady. I have lived in her castle for over six months and am truly honored and privileged to be considered her friend! She is a very talented poet in her own right however she has dedicated her life to the translation and teaching of Pound's epic "The Cantos" and also the upkeep of a vast library concerning the life of Pound.

Now return to the small canal. Turn right and you will see bridge 259. Cross this bridge and walk straight. When you are forced to turn left, walk a short distance and you will arrive at a small canal. Look to your right and there you will find bridge 260. Cross bridge 260. You will reach bridge 261 after winding along a narrow street and then by a canal. Do not cross bridge 261. Veer slightly to the right, passing a short alley on the right, and then arriving in the Campo S. Vio courtyard.

Walk to the right in this courtyard and you will arrive at bridge 262 very near the Grand Canal. Do not cross this bridge. Look to your left and you will see bridge 263. Cross this bridge and turn left. Up ahead will be bridge 264. Cross it and turn right. Walk straight until the street ends at a large body of water (the Giudecca Canal).

Bridge 265 is on the right and number 266 is on the left. Walk to bridge 266. Do not cross it. Turn around and walk across bridge 265. You are now on the street named Fondamenta Záttere ai Gesuati. Continue walking along Fondamenta Záttere ai Gesuati until you reach the next bridge. This is bridge 267 and the last bridge on this tour. Do not cross the bridge. Just before reaching this bridge you will find the Záttere Ponte Lungo vaporetto stop. This stop is the end of Tour 17.

For another quick side trip turn right just before the steps of bridge 267. Walk along the small canal and after only a few steps look across this canal. There you will see a gondola repair yard. This yard has remained basically the same as it was around 1900.

If you are fond of "Gelato" (Italian ice cream), one of the most famous places to buy it in Venice is located just prior to reaching bridge 267. Look for the name "gelati Nico". One taste and you will be glad you took the time to stop!

Tour 18, Bridges 268 – 281

This tour is composed of 14 bridges. The tour starts at the Záttere Ponte Lungo vaporetto stop and finishes at the Ca' Rezzónico vaporetto stop. As you leave the vaporetto, turn left and cross bridge 267 (from Tour 17). Immediately turn right and follow this winding street to bridge 268. Cross it and turn left. Bridge 269 will be on your left. To the right is bridge 276. Do not cross number 269. Walk back toward bridge 268, turning left into the Campo San Trováso courtyard. Walk to the far right corner of this courtyard. Now walk along side the canal and bridge 270 is on the right.

Cross bridge 270 and turn left. Bridge 271 is ahead on the left. Cross this bridge and then take the second right turn. Bridge 272 will soon appear. Do not cross this bridge. As you face the bridge, look left and you will see bridge 273. Do not cross bridge 273. Turn right at this bridge and you will soon arrive at bridge 274. Do not cross this bridge. Turn left and walk along side the canal on your right.

After a short walk beside this canal you will come to bridge 275. Do not cross this bridge. Just beyond bridge 275 is the restaurant "Locanda Montin". This restaurant was frequented by Ernest Hemingway and Ezra Pound. Just past the restaurant is bridge 276 on the right.

Cross number 276 and walk along side the canal on your left. Bridges 277 and 278 will soon appear. Do not cross them. Continue walking beside the canal and very shortly you will arrive at bridge 279. Do not cross this bridge either. Walk further along side the canal and bridge 280 will be in front of you.

Cross bridge 280 and walk until you arrive at another canal. On the left is bridge 251 (in Tour 16). Turn right at the canal and walk to the next bridge. This is bridge 250 (also in Tour 16). Turn right at this bridge onto Calle de L' Avogaría. This street will lead you to bridge 281. Cross bridge 281 and walk straight. Soon you will arrive at the Grand Canal and the Ca' Rezzónico vaporetto stop. This is the end of Tour 18.

Three bridges

Railing on bridge 281

Tour 19, Bridges 282 – 301

This tour has 20 bridges within it. These bridges are not as close together as is found in many of the other tours. Therefore this excursion involves a greater amount of walking than the average bridge tour. Tour 19 starts at the Ca' Rezzónico vaporetto stop and ends at the Piazzale Roma vaporetto stop.

Upon exiting the vaporetto, walk away from the Grand Canal. When you arrive at the San Bárnaba church, walk to the right around the front of it. There you will encounter bridge 282 on the right. Cross it and immediately turn left. Bridge 283 will be ahead. This bridge and the squares connected by it were used by rival clans to stage fist fights during part of the 1600's. Many people died as a result of the fighting. In 1705 a ban was imposed that stopped the fist fighting.

Cross bridge 283 and turn right. Stroll along side the canal until you reach bridge 284. Cross this bridge and walk straight. You will pass a church on your left. Then a white church will appear in front of you. Walk to the left and you will see bridge 285.

Do not cross bridge 285. Continue along side the canal on your right. You will soon reach bridge 286. Cross it and turn right. Now as you walk along the other side of the canal you will cross bridge 287. Continue walking straight along side the canal. First you will cross bridge 288 and then bridge 289 will be on the right. Do not cross bridge 289. Walk a little further along side the canal and you will arrive at bridge 290.

Cross bridge 290 and walk straight until the street turns right. Now after a few steps turn left. On the left side of this large courtyard is Santa Margherita church. Several good restaurants are located in this courtyard.

Walk beyond the Santa Margherita church and you will discover bridge 291. Cross this bridge. On your left bridge 292 will appear. Cross bridge 292 and then walk to the far left corner of the courtyard. As you exit the courtyard turn right at the first street. After a brief walk you will be at bridge 293. Do not cross this bridge. Turn around and walk straight until you arrive at bridge 294. Do not cross this bridge either.

Continue walking along side the canal and the next bridge is number 295. Cross this bridge. On your right is bridge 296. Walk past bridge 296 without crossing it. As you walk along side the canal on your right you will soon arrive at bridge 297 on your right and bridge 233 (from Tour 15) straight ahead. Cross bridge 297.

Walk along side the canal and bridge 298 will be ahead. Do not cross bridge 298. Turn right at this bridge and after a nice stroll through a small park you will arrive at bridge 299. Do not cross this bridge. Turn left at the bridge and enjoy a pleasant stroll along side this canal that leads to the Grand Canal. At the intersection of this canal and the Grand Canal is bridge 300. Do not cross this bridge. Turn left and enjoy the sights as you walk along side the Grand Canal. Soon you will reach bridge 301, the final bridge on this tour. Cross bridge 301 and then just ahead is the Piazzale Roma vaporetto stop. This is the end of Tour 19.

Railing on bridge 282

Tour 20, Bridges 302 – 313

This tour contains 12 bridges. The tour begins at the Ferrovia degli Scalzi vaporetto stop and ends at the San Stae vaporetto stop. Exit the vaporetto and turn right, walking along side the Grand Canal. The Ponte degli Scalzi bridge (bridge 224 in Tour 14) is just ahead. Cross this bridge and walk straight ahead. Just before the street ends turn left. Bridge 302 crosses a small canal. Cross this bridge and turn right along side the canal. A short walk will lead you to bridge 303. Cross this bridge and walk straight. Go to the end of the street and bridge 304 will be on your left.

Cross bridge 304 and turn right. You will soon arrive at bridge 305. Do not cross number 305. Continue walking along side the canal and bridge 306 will appear. Do not cross this bridge. Turn around and go back past bridge 305. Then cross bridge 304 again. Take the first right turn. You will arrive back at bridge 303. Do not cross bridge 303. Turn right and on your left will be bridge 307.

Cross bridge 307. Walk straight and soon you will enter a small courtyard named Campo d. Strope. Walk along the right side of this courtyard and take the second street on the right. Shortly you will be forced to turn left. Soon after making this turn bridge 308 will appear.

Cross bridge 308 and then turn left at the first opportunity. You will enter a courtyard with a church in the center. On your left will be two bridges, numbers 309 and 310. Bridge 310 is beside the church. Do not cross either bridge. Walk around the church until you reach a canal. An un-numbered (and un-photographed) bridge is on the left. Bridge 311 is directly in front of you.

Cross bridge 311. Soon you will be forced to turn right. Go until this street ends, then turn right again. Take a left turn, then the first right turn. Now veer to the right. Another bridge will appear that was not photographed or numbered. Cross this bridge. Stay to the right side as you walk through a courtyard. Upon entering a street continue walking to the right. This leads to bridge 312. Cross this bridge and turn left.

Take the first right turn. Bridge 313 is just ahead. This is the last bridge on this tour. Cross bridge 313 and take the second left turn. Now walk to the Grand Canal. You will be at the San Stae vaporetto stop which is the end of Tour 20.

Railing on bridge 302

Railing on bridge 307

Tour 21, Bridges 314 – 335

This tour is composed of 22 bridges. Tour 21 starts and ends at the San Stae vaporetto stop. The San Stae church is located here. If the door is unlocked, a visit to this beautiful church is certainly worth your time. Stand with the vaporetto to your back. Walk to the left of the church. There you will find bridge 314. Cross this bridge.

Turn right. Bridge 315 will appear. Do not cross this bridge. Up ahead is bridge 316 on the right. Walk past this bridge and you will see bridge 317. Do not cross this bridge. Turn left at bridge 317 and walk straight through the small courtyard to bridge 318. Do not cross bridge 318. Turn around and walk back toward bridge 317. Look to the left of bridge 317 and you will see bridge 319.

You can not cross bridge 319. Cross bridge 317 and turn left. Go to the third street on the right, Ramo Carminati. Turn onto this street. Bridge 320 will soon appear. Do not cross bridge 320. Turn around and take the second right. This street will lead you to bridge 321. Cross bridge 321 and walk straight until you can turn left. Make this turn and then after a few steps turn left again. This street will lead to bridge 322. Do not cross bridge 322.

Turn around at bridge 322. Take the first right. Now instead of turning right and going back to bridge 321, continue walking straight and you will see bridge number 323. Cross this bridge and ahead you will observe bridge 324. Cross this bridge and take the second left turn. Then take the first right turn and you will see bridge 325.

Do not cross bridge 325. Turn around and take the first right turn. This street is Calle Del Cristo. This street will lead to bridge 326. Cross bridge 326 and take the second right. After a very short walk you will arrive at bridge 327. Cross it and walk straight until you arrive at bridge 328. Do not cross bridge 328. Turn around and walk back to bridge 327, which will be straight ahead. Without crossing bridge 327, turn right and walk along side the canal. When the street ends, walk around the building, staying to the left. Bridge 329 will be discovered once you get back to the canal. Do not cross bridge 329.

With bridge 329 to your back, walk away from the bridge and then take the first left turn. Now take the first right turn and you will arrive at bridge 330. As you cross bridge 330 you will see bridge 331 on your left. Do not cross bridge 331. Walk on past it to the next bridge, number 332. Cross bridge 332 and then take the next right. Now take the first left.

This leads to bridge 333. Cross this bridge and walk a short distance to bridge 334. Do not cross this bridge. Turn right at the bridge and then up ahead you will see bridge 335. This is the last bridge on this tour. Cross bridge 335 and walk to the next canal. Turn right at this canal. Cross bridge 314. You are now at the Grand Canal and the San Stae vaporetto stop. This is the end of Tour 21.

Railing on bridge 317

This tour contains 10 bridges. The tour begins at the Rialto vaporetto stop and terminates at the San Silvestro vaporetto stop. Exit the vaporetto and turn left along side the Grand Canal. Cross the beautiful 16th century Rialto Bridge (bridge 75 in Tour 4). Once you leave the bridge you will be in the famous Rialto District.

The Rialto Markets are famous for their colorfulness and wide range of merchandise. Visit the fresh produce and fish markets early in the morning for an unforgettable experience.

Turn right and walk along side the Grand Canal. Stay as close to the water as possible. You will arrive at bridge 336 just after you pass the fish market. Cross bridge 336. Take the first turn to the left. Then take the next left turn and you will arrive at bridges 337 and 338. Bridge 337 is on your left and number 338 is straight ahead. Do not cross either bridge. With bridge 338 to your back, walk straight and take the second left. After a short walk take the first left turn. This leads to bridge 339.

Cross bridge 339. Take the third right turn. Now follow the curve to the left. This street will take you to bridge 340. Cross this bridge and turn left, walking along side the small canal. Soon you will find yourself at bridge 341. Cross this bridge and take the first right. Keep winding your way to the right and you will arrive at bridge 342. Cross this bridge and you will enter a very large courtyard, Campo San Polo. Walk toward the San Polo church.

Stay on the left side of the church and walk to the rear of it. There you will discover bridge 343. Do not cross bridge 343. Turn around and take the first street on the right near the church. At the first opportunity to turn left, do so. This street will take you to bridge 344. Do not cross this bridge.

Turn around and go back to the church. Now turn right. Continue walking along the right side of the courtyard and straight ahead you will see bridge 345. Cross this bridge. Keep walking straight and you will arrive at a very wide, low bridge. Watch closely or you will not realize it is a bridge. No picture was taken of this bridge.

Two different streets lead away from the bridge on the other side. Take the street on the right. Walk straight for a short distance and you will enter a small courtyard named Campo San Aponàl. As you enter the courtyard turn right. Turn on the street named Calle Dei Sbianchesini. Walk straight until you reach the Grand Canal. On the right is the San Silvestro vaporetto stop. This is the end of Tour 22.

Railings on bridge 337 and one other

Railing on bridge 338

Tour 23, Bridges 346 – 356

This tour contains 11 bridges. The tour starts and ends at the San Tomà vaporetto stop. As you leave the vaporetto take the first left turn. After a brief walk you will approach bridge 346. This bridge, Ponte De La Frescada, was partially constructed in the latter part of the eighth century. Do not cross this bridge.

Turn right just before the entrance to the bridge and walk along side the canal. The next bridge is number 347. Cross this bridge and walk straight. Soon you will arrive at bridge 348. Do not cross this bridge. Turn around and then take the first street to the left. Now take the second turn to the right. Soon bridge 349 will appear.

Do not cross bridge 349. Turn around. Take the first right and then the second right. Now you will be at bridge 350. Cross this bridge. Turn right and then left. You will arrive in a courtyard with a white church on the left and a huge church on the right. Walk all the way to the end of the church on the right. Now turn left and you will discover bridge 351.

Cross bridge 351 and turn right. A brief walk along side the canal will get you to bridge 352. Turn around and walk back to bridge 351. Continue walking straight, leaving bridge 351 on your left. Bridge 353 is just ahead. Cross this bridge and turn right. After a few steps turn left onto Calle De La Chiesa. After you leave the canal take the first right turn. Now take the second right turn. A short walk will take you to bridge 354.

Cross bridge 354. On your left is bridge 355. Do not cross this bridge. Turn around and go back over bridge 354. You will arrive in Campo S. Stin (a large sign also reads Sestier De S. Polo). Turn left on Calle De La Chiesa. Now you will again see bridge 353. Cross it and then cross bridge 351 on the right.

You are now back in the courtyard of the huge church you visited just a short while ago. Walk straight past the church to the other end of it. Now turn left onto the street named Calle Larga (which can be located by the "Al Vaporetto" sign). When forced to make a turn, turn right and then immediately turn left. Stay to the left as you approach San Tomà church. You are in the Campo San Tomà courtyard.

Walk around the left side of the church. When you come upon a very small private bridge, bypass it. Continue beyond the church and you will discover bridge 356. Do not cross this bridge. Go back to the church and walk to the front of it. Continue past the church on Calle Del Campaniel Detta Civran O Grimani. Take the first left turn. This street takes you to the San Tomà vaporetto stop, the end of this tour.

Railing on bridge 351

Railing on bridge 354

This tour is comprised of 7 bridges on the island of Giudecca. The tour begins at the Redentore vaporetto stop and finishes at the Palanca vaporetto stop. There is a considerable amount of walking involved in this tour. The distance is approximately 1,800 meters. Once you exit the vaporetto, turn left and walk along side the water's edge of the large Giudecca canal.

The famous Redentore church is located here. The exterior of this church has many features that were modeled after the Pantheon in Rome. On the third weekend of each July, the Feast of the Redeemer is celebrated by using boats to form a bridge across the Giudecca canal from the Redentore church to the main island of Venice.

You will soon reach bridge 357. Do not cross this bridge. Turn right just before the bridge and you will soon be walking along side a small canal. Up ahead will be bridge 358. Do not cross this bridge. Turn around and go back to the Giudecca canal.

Turn left at the Giudecca canal and stroll along the street, passing the Redentore vaporetto stop. As you continue walking along side the canal you will come upon bridge 359. Cross this bridge and take the first left. This street will lead to bridge 360. Cross this bridge and walk straight, having the wider canal on your left. Take the third right turn onto Calle Junghans. Walk straight and soon you will arrive at bridge 361.

Do not cross bridge 361. Turn around and walk away from the bridge. Take the first left under the building. At the canal turn right. Bridge 362 is on your left. Cross this bridge and walk straight. Soon you will be back at the Giudecca canal. Turn left at the canal and then you will cross bridge 363. This is the last bridge on the tour. Continue walking along side the Giudecca canal until you arrive at the Palanca vaporetto stop. This marks the end of Tour 24 and the start of Tour 25.

Redentore church

This tour contains 7 bridges on the island of Giudecca. The tour begins at the Palanca vaporetto stop and ends at the Sacca Fisola vaporetto stop. This tour involves considerable walking. When leaving the vaporetto turn right and walk along side the Giudecca canal until you come to bridge 364. Cross it and continue your stroll beside the Giudecca canal eventually arriving at bridge 365.

Do not cross bridge 365. Turn around and go back to bridge 364. Immediately after crossing bridge 364 turn right and you will see bridge 366 ahead. Walk on past bridge 366 without crossing it. Continue walking straight and you will come to bridge 367. Cross this bridge and walk along side the canal on your right. You will soon arrive at bridge 368.

Do not cross bridge 368. Walk past it and continue straight for about 200 meters. You will arrive at bridge 369. Cross it and keep walking straight until you reach bridge 370. Cross this bridge and follow the street that leads straight away from the canal. Take the first right turn onto Calle Del Fisola. Now you will see the Sacca Fisola vaporetto stop ahead. This is the end of Tour 25.

San Donato church at bridge 375

This tour contains 9 bridges. These bridges are all located on the island of Murano. The tour begins at the Venièr vaporetto stop and ends at the Colonna vaporetto stop. Exit the vaporetto stop and walk straight away from it on Calle Barovier.

After the street turns to the right, take the third left turn onto Calle Motta. At the end of this street turn left. Then take the first right turn onto Calle De L' Artigiano. This street veers to the right. Then you will see a sign named Calle Angelo Zaniol. Turn left here. Bridge 371 will be on your right.

Do not cross bridge 371. Turn around and veer to the left. Here you will find bridge 372. Cross this bridge and turn right. Walk along side the canal and soon bridge 373 will appear. Do not cross this bridge. Continue your stroll along side the canal and after a short walk you will cross bridge 374. Up ahead you will see bridge 375.

Cross bridge 375 and turn left. Now enjoy your stroll along side the canal. After a long stroll bridge 376 will appear up ahead. Cross bridge 376 and turn left. Now you will see bridge 377. Cross this bridge and turn right. Walk beside the canal and you will soon arrive at bridge 378. Do not cross this bridge. Continue walking beside the canal. Now you will come to the last bridge on this tour, bridge 379. Cross this bridge and turn left. After a short walk you will arrive at the Colonna vaporetto stop. This is the end of tour 26.

Leaning Tower on the Island of Burano

This tour is composed of 13 bridges. Tour 27 includes bridges on the islands of Burano, Mazzorbo and Torcello. The tour starts and ends on the island of Burano at the vaporetto stop named Burano. Exit the vaporetto and turn left. Walk beside the water's edge. Continue straight even when the walkway narrows. Turn right at the fuel pumps and the small canal. After a short walk you will be at bridge 380.

Cross bridge 380 and turn right and then immediately turn left. Continue straight. You will pass a round tower on the right. As you continue straight you will reach a small canal. Turn right. This will lead you to bridge 381 on your left. Do not cross bridge 381. Turn right at this bridge. Take a left and then a right. This takes you to a courtyard with a church on the left.

You can see a leaning tower at one end of this courtyard. Stay on the right side of the courtyard. As you exit this courtyard you will see a street named Rio terrà Pizzo that turns to the left. Follow this street. Take the first right turn off this street under a low archway. You will arrive at a canal and see bridge 382.

Cross bridge 382 and turn right. Walk along side the canal and after a while you will arrive at bridge 383. Go to the top of this bridge and turn to the right, walking down the steps. Walk along side the canal. Soon bridge 384 will appear. Don't cross this bridge. Continue along side the canal. Soon a wooden bridge, number 385 will appear on the left.

Cross bridge 385 and walk back to bridge 384. Go to the second street past bridge 384 and turn right. This is in the bend of the canal. As the street opens up into a wide grassy area, veer to the left and you will soon see the Burano vaporetto stop.

The island of Mazzorbo is to the left of the vaporetto stop. In the distant past this island was used to house exiles. Mazzorbo is connected to Burano by a wooden bridge. This is bridge number 386. Cross this bridge and look to the left. You will see bridge 387 ahead of you. Cross this bridge and take the left fork of the walkway. The last two bridges on this island will require approximately a fifteen minute roundtrip walk. Follow the walkway and eventually you will pass a pink-walled cemetery on your right.

Turn right at the end of the wall. Follow the stone walkway to the canal and then turn left. Bridge 388 will soon come into view. Do not cross this bridge. Turn around and you will see bridge 389 in the opposite direction. Do not cross bridge 389 either. Leave the canal and retrace your steps back to bridge 387. Cross this bridge and also bridge 386 (the bridge connecting the islands of Burano and Mazzorbo). Now walk to the Burano vaporetto stop.

Locate the dock that services the vaporetto to Torcello. This is a short boat ride, requiring only five minutes. The first inhabitants of Venice settled on Torcello. Now the island is remote, with only two bridges. The island does have a very nice restaurant and an ambiance all its own.

Upon reaching the Torcello vaporetto stop, veer to the right along a brick walkway and a small canal. You will soon arrive at bridge 390, Ponte del Diavolo. This bridge is known as the "devils bridge". The bridge was constructed with no railings along the side. Fist fights often occurred on the bridge, with the loser being knocked into the canal. Notice the stone and brick surface of the bridge. Walk past it and continue along the canal. As this lovely waterway curves to the left you will see bridge 391. This is the last bridge on the tour. Now you must return to the Torcello vaporetto stop, take the boat to Burano, and then return to the main islands of Venice.

Steps of the devil's bridge

Photographs of the Bridges

1 Della Paglia   2 dei Sospiri

3   4

5   6

7   8

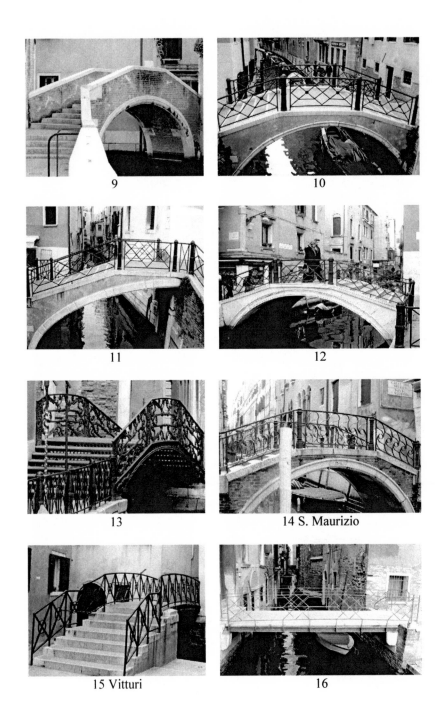

9

10

11

12

13

14 S. Maurizio

15 Vitturi

16

17

18 Giustinian

19

20 dell' Accademia

21

22

23

24 De L' Albero

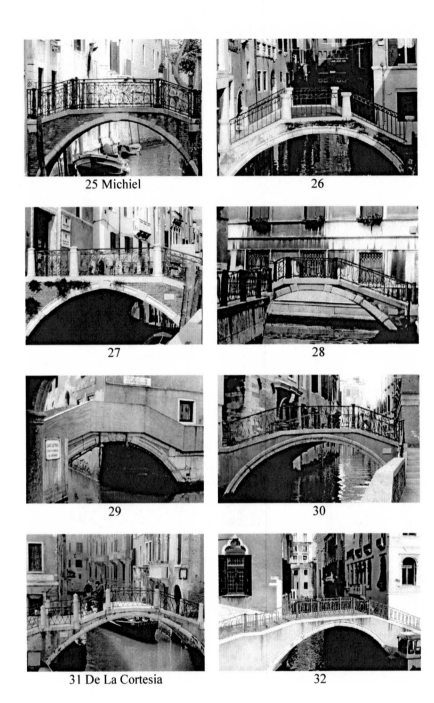

25 Michiel

26

27

28

29

30

31 De La Cortesia

32

94

33   34 Dei Fuseri

35   36 De Piscina

37 De Le Colonne   38

39   40 Dei Dai

41

42

43 De Le Balote

44 De Le Pignate

45 Del Lovo

46

47

48

49

50 De La Malvasia

51

52 De La Guerra

53

54

55

56

57

58

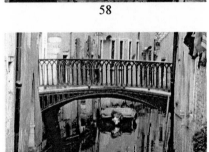

59 Dei Carmini

60 De La Corona

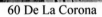

61 Storto

62

63

64 Pasqualigo E Avogadro

65

66

67

68

69

70 De Rugagiuffa

71 De Le Bande

72 Del Mondo Novo

99

73 De La Fava

74 S. Antonio

75 del Rialto

76 De L'Olio

77 Marco Polo

78 Del Pistor

79

80

81

82 Del Paradiso

83 Dei Preti

84 Marcello O Pindemonte

85 Borgoloco

86 Tetta

87 Cappello

88 S. Lorenzo

89 Novo   90 S. Severo

91 Lion   92 Dei Greci

93   94 Del Diavolo

95 De La Pieta'   96 Del Sepolcro

97 De La Pieta'

98 S. Antonia

99 De La Comenda

100 De La Corte Nova

101 Del Fontego

102 De S. Francesco O Del Nuncio

103 De S Francesco O Del Nescio

104 Del Suffragio O Del Cristo

105 De La Scoazzera

106 Dei Scudi

107 De L'Arco

108 De La Grana

109 Storto

110 Dei Penini

111 De L' Inferno

112 Del Purgatorio

113 Erizzo

114 Ca Di Dio

115

116

117 De L'Arsenal O Del Paradiso

118

119 De La Tana

120 Nuovo

121 S. Gioachin

122 Rielo

123

124 S. Ana

125

126

127

128 S. I Sepo

129

130

131

132

133

134

135 Novo S. Felice

136 Ubaldo Belli

137 Privli

138

139

140 S. Caterina

141 Molin De La Racheta

142 S. Andrea

143 Corrente

144 De Le Vele

108

145 Priuli

146

147 S. Giovanni Grisostomo

148

149 Giustinian

150 Dei Sartori

151 De L' Acquavita

152 Dei Gesuiti

153 Dona'

154 Panada

155 Mendicanti

156 Cavallo

157 De La Panada

158 Del Piovan O Del Volto

159 S. Maria Novo

160 Widmann

161 Pasqualigo

162 Dei Miracoli

163

164 E Calle De Le Erbe

165 Del Cristo

166

167 Dei Conzafelzi

168 De L' Ospealeto

111

169

170

171 Fondamenta Di S. Giustina

172

173 dei Tre Archi

174 del Batelo

175

176 De Canaregio

177 De Gheto Vechio

178 De Gheto Novo

179 De Gheto Novo

180 De Le Torete

181 S. Girolamo

182 De Le Capuzzine

183 Moro

184

185 Contarini

186 Turlona

187 Bonaventura

188 S. Alvise

189 De La Malvasia

190 Dei Ormesini

191 Loredan

192 De L' Aseo

193 Dei Lustraferi

194

195 Del Forno

196 Rosso O Dei Trasti

197 Brazzo

198 Dei Mori

199 Dei Muti

200 De La Saca

201 De La Madona De L'Orto

202 Storto

203 De L' Anconeta

204

205 Correr

206 De L' Ogio

207 Nicolo Pasovaligo

208 Vendramin

209 S. Fosca

210 S. Antonio

211 Diedo

212 Moro

213 Zancani

214

215 Corte Vechia

215, another picture

217 De La Misericordia   218

219   220 De La Crea

221   222

223   224 degli Scalzi

225

226

227 De S. Maria Maggior

228

229 De Ca' Rizzi

230

231

232 Del Pagan

233

234 De La Cereria

235 De La Sbiaca

236

237

238

239 Dei Guardiani

240

241 Storto

242 De La Madona

243

244 De Le Terese

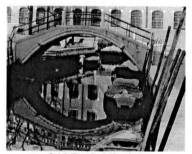

245 De S. Nicolo'

246

247

248

249 De La Madalena

250 De S. Sebastian

251 De S. Basegio

252 Mounn

253 Dell' Abazia

254

255

256 Del Umilta'

257

258

259

260 S. Cristoforo

261 Del Formager

262

263

264

265 Deilina Calcina

266

267 Longo

268 De La Scoasera

269 Trevisan

270 S. Trovaso

271 Delle Maravegie

272 Del Squero

273 Lombardo

274 Delle Turchette

275

276

277

278

279 Sartorio

280

281 Ognisanti

282 S. Barnaba

283 Dei Pugni

284

285 Foscarini

286 Del Socorso

287 Briati

288

289 Del Forno

290

291

292 S. Pantalon

293 Vinanti

294 Marcello

295 Del Gafaro

296 Dei Squartai

297

298

299 Dei Tolentini

300

301

302 De La Berg

303 Cappello O Dei Garzoti

304 Canal

305

306 De Le Sechere

307 Del Cristo

308 De Le Oche

309 De L' Anatomia

310 Ruga Bella O Del Forner

311 Del Savio

312 Del Megio

313 Del Tentor

314 Giovanelli

315

316

317 De La Rioda

318 Del Cristo O Del Tentor

319

320 Colombo

321 Storto

322 Del Modena

323 S. Boldo

324 Del Parucheta

325 Bernardo

326 Del Forner

327 De L' Agnella

328 De Le Tette

329 S. Maria Mater Domini　　　330 Giovanni Andrea De La Croce

331　　　　　　　　　　　332 De La Chiesa

333 Del Ravano　　　　　　　334 Del Forner

335 Pesaro　　　　　　　　　336

337 De Le Becarie

338 De Le Do Spade

339 Raspi O Sansoni

340 Storto

341 De La Furatola

342 Cavalli

343 S. Polo

344 Dei Meloni

345 De La Madoneta

346 De La Frescada

347

348 Foscari

349 S. Rocco

350 Della Scuola

351 Dei Frari

352

353 S. Stin

354 De Ca' Dona'

355 S.Agostin

356 Del Traghetto

357 De La Croce

358

359 Longo

360 S. Angelo

135

361 De Le Scuole

362 De La Palada

363 Picolo

364 S. Eufemia

365

366

367 Lagoscuro

368

369

370 Dei Lavraneri

371

372 Angelo Zaniol

373 De Le Terese

374 S. Martin

375 S. Donato

376 Longo

377 S. Pietro Martire · · · · · · · · · · · · 378 De Mezo

379 S. Chiara · · · · · · · · · · · · 380

381 · · · · · · · · · · · · 382

383 · · · · · · · · · · · · 384

385

386

387

388

389

390 del Diavolo

391

392 di Calatrava

Some Interesting Bridge Facts

The bridges of Venice can be categorized based on various criteria. One classification is the material used to construct the primary section of the bridge. Another categorization is the type of railing used.

One hundred fifty one bridges are constructed of brick and stone and have metal railings. One hundred forty bridges are made entirely of brick and stone. Venice has forty eight bridges that are metal. Bridges made of wood make up forty three bridges of the total.

Bridge 140 has a very low railing. Bridge 390 (the devil's bridge) has no railing at all. The Bridge Of Sighs and the Rialto Bridge are both covered bridges. Some bridges have locked gates on them so you are unable to cross these structures. A few bridges lead to a locked door and are therefore private as well. Three bridges are directly related to Italy's most famous epic poem, the *Divine Comedy* by Dante. These bridges are Ponte De L' Inferno, Ponte Del Purgatorio, and Ponte Del Paradiso (numbers 111, 112, and 82 respectively). During one of Dante's visits to Venice he took note of workers using hot black tar. This site inspired him to write part of the "*Inferno*".

Another interesting aspect of Venice's bridges is that some of them have identical names. Six bridges have the name Ponte Storto. Three bridges are named Ponte Longo. Each of the following bridge names are used on two bridges; S. Antonio, De La Pieta', De Gheto Novo, De La Malvasia, Del Forno, and Del Cristo. This is not a complete list, but you get the idea!

As mentioned earlier, a few of the bridges are not included in this book. The primary reason is that some bridges and canals were under renovation and therefore unavailable to photograph. Examples of this work can be seen in the pictures of bridges 209, 210 and 211 as well as the picture on page 64.

My other book, "Venice Bridges, A Pictorial Collection", includes full color photographs of the bridges listed in this book. The vivid color photographs are housed in an 8 by 10 volume and make a beautiful "coffee-table" book. In almost every case the bridge pictures are presented two per page. The color photographs bring out the intrinsic beauty of these centuries old structures.

Travel Information and Tips

This section is intended to be only a brief introduction concerning a visit to Venice. Detailed information can be found in numerous travel publications devoted to this fascinating city.

Upon arrival in Venice, one obvious difference compared to other cities is that transportation within the city is limited to walking and boating. No motorized wheeled vehicles are permitted beyond the main parking lot. This rule also applies to bicycles as well. These rules create a very quiet and safe city. Unpleasant noise comes primarily from the hordes of people found in the very popular areas of St. Mark's Square, Rialto Bridge, and the main shopping streets between these two districts.

Venice is a city made for walking. Numerous points of interest can be found as you turn practically every corner. Walking becomes unpleasant only when confronted with large numbers of people or undesirable weather. Negotiating narrow alleyways with umbrellas open is a challenge when meeting other "open umbrellas".

Boats seem to be everywhere in Venice. The cheapest way to travel by boat is the vaporetto. This mode of transportation is equivalent to bus lines in a normal city. These boats become very crowded during the high tourist season. Vaporetto ticket prices as of the early part of 2008 are as follows (in Euros for 1 person): One hour = €6.5 (one way), 12 hours = €14, 24 hours = €16, 36 hours = €21, 48 hours = €26, and 72 hours = €31. These prices are subject to change. If you are caught riding a vaporetto without a ticket you will be charged the price of a normal ticket plus a fine of at least €30!

Water taxis are also available. These boats are more expensive than the vaporetto. They function practically the same as normal taxis. The most expensive mode of water travel is the famed gondola. Human powered, these vessels are world famous for their beauty and romantic atmosphere (especially at night quietly slipping through the narrow canals as light reflects off the water).

A "poor-mans" gondola ride can easily be accomplished by utilizing the Traghetto (ferry system) of Venice. These older, less glamorous gondolas cross the Grand Canal at approximately seven locations.

Here are a few tips on eating in Venice. In areas where tourists congregate, restaurants frequently have higher prices, lower quality food, and less friendly (and/or more obstinate) wait staff. I visited one restaurant on the waterfront in the Rialto area that vividly proves my point. When I requested to share an entrée with another person, we were told this was not allowed. And we were told this fact in a very stern manner, as if to imply what fools we were for not knowing this!

If you sit down at a table with a tablecloth, you can expect to pay at least €4 more for a seating charge. Choose a table without a tablecloth (usually near the front of the restaurant)! Remember that a service charge of at least 12% is usually automatically added to your bill. Some restaurants will lure you in with "cheap" food prices listed on sidewalk menus. Once you sit down to order, be sure you are aware of the drink prices. Often these prices will be inflated to compensate for the "lower" food prices.

Practically everyone loves Italian gelato. Be aware if that is all you order, and you sit down at one of the restaurant's tables (even outdoors), you may be asked to leave. When sitting down for a full meal, be aware that the small basket of bread automatically brought to your table before your entrée may cost you 3 to 4 Euros. And finally, remember the cups of coffee you get will be very small, even if you ask for "American style" coffee. And drink refills are not free!

On a positive note, the Train Station is a great place to get a quick, reasonable meal. There is a cafeteria-style line on the right. On the left side are numerous Italian "sandwiches". First you look at the "sandwiches" and decide what you want. Note the price of this item. Now go to the cashier near the main door and pay for the item. He/she will give you a receipt. Take this receipt back to the food counter and tell the person behind the counter what you want and give them the receipt. It sounds complicated but it really is not.

Another very good cafeteria-style restaurant is located less than a five minute walk from the train station. As you exit the station walk to your left along the busy street lined with shops of all sorts. The restaurant is named "Brek" and is on the left side of the street. As of my last visit there very few servers spoke English, but that should not deter you. Stand back a moment and observe how customers order and pay for their food. It's not complicated and the food and prices are very satisfactory.

Venice has numerous wonderful restaurants. Being aware of the tips listed above will make your eating experience more enjoyable. Buon Appetito!

Web Sites

www.turismovenezia.it/eng   (official site of the Venice Tourist Board)
www.savevenice.org
www.veniceinperil.org
www.jamesbroos.com

Web Cams

turismovenezia.it/eng
camsturion.com
http://turismo.regione.veneto.it/webcam/webcam2.html

Note: Using your favorite Internet search engine will result in hundreds of additional informative web sites concerning Venice.

Acknowledgments

I wish to express my appreciation to the following individuals in the completion of this book:

To my wife for her support and understanding, to the other members of my family and friends who provided encouragement, to Mary de Rachewiltz for her inspiration and for permission to use Ezra Pound's (her father's) poem *Night Litany*, and to Doctor Karl B. Fields for keeping me healthy.

Index

Accademia, 20, 34, 35, 36, 93
Accademia Galleria, 34, 36
Alguibario café, 52
Arsenale, 33, 45, 46, 47
Bridge of Fists, 28
Bridge of Sighs, 19, 21, 34, 35, 40
Burano, 13, 14, 33, 86, 87, 88
Ca' d' Oro, 34, 60
Café Florian, 10, 34, 40
Campanile, 34
devil's bridge, 29, 140
Doge's Palace, 19, 34, 35
Ernest Hemingway, 69
Ezra Pound, 5, 67, 69, 144
Ferrovia, 12, 33, 34, 61, 73
Gelato, 14, 39, 68
Giovanni Paolo church, 53
Giudecca, 10, 33, 68, 81, 83
Gondola Repair Shop, 34
Grand Canal, 12, 21, 22, 27, 30, 36, 39, 60, 61, 63, 65, 68, 69, 71, 72,
    73, 74, 76, 77, 78
handmade lace, 13
home made cosmetics, 60
Italian ice cream, 68
Jewish Ghetto, 34
La Fenice, 34, 37, 38
La Fenice Opera House, 34
La Pietà church, 11, 45
leaning tower, 13, 37, 87
Madonna dell'Orto Church, 34
Map, 32
Marco Polo, 10, 13, 15, 34, 43, 100
Mary de Rachewiltz, 67, 144
Merceria, 39

Murano, 13, 85
Murano glass, 13
Palazzo Ducale, 34
Peggy Guggenheim, 34
Piazzale Roma, 12, 33, 34, 63, 65, 71, 72
Ponte Accademia, 15, 20
Ponte De L' Arco, 25
Ponte degli Scalzi, 17, 27, 61, 62, 73
Ponte Dei Pugni, 17, 28
Ponte Dei Sospiri, 15, 19
Ponte Dei Tre Archi, 26
Ponte del Diavolo, 18, 29, 88
Ponte Del Paradiso, 15, 24
Ponte di Calatrava, 12, 18, 30
quick, reasonable meal, 142
Redentore, 10, 33, 34, 81, 82
Rialto, 9, 12, 15, 21, 22, 33, 34, 35, 39, 41, 42, 43, 77, 100, 140, 141, 142
San Stae church, 75
Santa Margherita church, 71
Santa Maria della Salute, 10, 34, 67
Santa Maria Formosa Church, 34
Santa Maria Gloriosa dei Frari Church, 34
Santo Stefano Church, 34
St. Mark's Basilica, 9, 34, 39
St. Mark's Square, 10, 11, 12, 34, 35, 37, 38, 39, 40, 43, 141
Table of Bridge Tours, 33
three bakeries, 51, 60
Tintoretto, 52, 67
Titian, 52, 67
Torcello, 13, 14, 29, 87, 88
Traghetto, 18, 135, 142
Vivaldi, 11, 14, 34, 45, 58
Web Cams, 144

CPSIA information can be obtained at www.ICGtesting.com
Printed in the USA
BVOW041420261212

309122BV00002B/510/P